IMPROVING

EMPLOYEE
PERFORMANCE

THROUGH

APPRAISAL

AND COACHING

Second Edition

IMPROVING

EMPLOYEE

PERFORMANCE

THROUGH

APPRAISAL

AND COACHING

Second Edition

Donald L. Kirkpatrick
Foreword by Dick Grote

⨝AMACOM

American Management Association

New York • Atlanta • Brussels • Chicago • Mexico City • San Francisco
Shanghai • Tokyo • Toronto • Washington, D.C.

This publication is designed to provide accurate and authoritative
information in regard to the subject matter covered. It is sold with the
understanding that the publisher is not engaged in rendering legal,
accounting, or other professional service. If legal advice or other expert
assistance is required, the services of a competent professional person
should be sought.

Library of Congress Cataloging-in-Publication Data

Kirkpatrick, Donald L.
    Improving employee performance through appraisal and coaching /
Donald L. Kirkpatrick ; foreword by Dick Grote. — 2nd ed.
        p.   cm.
    Rev. ed. of: How to improve performance through appraisal and coaching.
    Includes bibliographical references and index.
    ISBN 0-8144-0876-1
    1. Employees—Rating of.   I. Kirkpatrick, Donald L. How to improve
performance through appraisal and coaching.   II. Title.

    HF5549.5.R3K54   2006
    658.3'125—dc22

                                                              2005025643

Printing number

10 9 8 7 6 5 4 3 2 1

Contents

Foreword

was going through the attic recently, sorting through some ancient files. In a pile of old magazines I ran across a tattered copy of ASTD's *Training and Development Journal* from 1971. I had saved it because in it was the first article I ever wrote about performance management. As I thumbed through it, I noticed that the masthead listed ASTD's regional vice presidents. There was Don Kirkpatrick's name.

At that time, thirty-five years ago, Don was already one of the most significant figures in the field of training and development. Today, nothing's changed. Don Kirkpatrick remains one of the most influential and thought-provoking thinkers and writers in the field of performance management and the development of human talent in organizations.

Most human resource management professionals are familiar with Don's contribution to the field of training and development through his development of what now is commonly referred to as "Kirkpatrick's Four Levels of Evaluation." Don observed that the evaluation of a training program's effectiveness begins with Level One—*Reaction*. How well did the participants like the program? But too many evaluation efforts don't go any further than a smile sheet. More important than how people felt about the program, Don told us, was Level Two—*Learning*. Did the participants learn the skills the program was designed to teach? Did they do better on the posttest than they did on the pretest? Regardless of how much they liked the program, did they actually acquire the skills the program intended to teach them?

But that's still not enough. While users may have liked the program and scored high on the final exam, the next level—*Behavior*—is much more important. Are the participants using what they learned back on the job? Have the trainees transferred their new skills and learnings to their everyday environment?

Finally—and here comes the bottom-line question—has all this effort made any difference? Yes, the salesmen liked the program. Yes, they learned all of the selling skills we taught them and, yes, they're using those skills when they call on their customers. But has this led to an increase in sales? That's Don's final level: *Results*. From a business and organizational perspective, it's only at the level of results that training programs pay off.

Don Kirkpatrick first presented his model in 1959 in a series of articles in the *Training and Development Journal*. Kirkpatrick's Four Levels of Evaluation is a model of profound simplicity. New trainers have a head-slapping experience and say, "Of course!" when they are first introduced to the four levels and the need to evaluate not just how much people liked the program and how much they learned but just what benefit the organization got out of making the investment in training them. Don revolutionized the field of training and development.

But this book isn't about training or evaluation. And it isn't written just for people in the training industry or the human resources field. This book may represent an even more important contribution, since it focuses on managing human performance throughout an organization. It is directed at operating managers who have to guide and coach and correct and motivate high performance. It's aimed at trainers who must teach managers how to meet their responsibilities for managing the performance of other people. And it is directed toward HR professionals who must make sure that the people-management side of the business happens as it's supposed to.

Based on the volume originally published in 1982, this updated and revised edition will help everyone involved with the management of human performance achieve excellence in this challenging area. It deals with issues that matter.

Improving Employee Performance Through Appraisal and Coaching is truthfully titled. It is a how-to book, not a theoretical treatise. It gives managers the skills they need to appraise performance honestly, accurately, and confidently.

When I served as subject-matter expert in a national benchmarking study of best practices in performance management a few years ago, I identified the companies that genuinely are doing outstanding work in their performance appraisal, assessment, and development efforts. But among these stellar organizations there was one common frustration. In spite of the fact that their systems were the best around, they still had trouble getting their managers to do a good job of setting goals. This book will help them solve this problem and show managers how to clarify what is expected of subordinates.

Grade inflation is one of the loudest complaints made about America's prestige universities. In fact, as I was reading an issue of *The Atlantic Monthly* recently, I found a dramatic chart illustrating the year-by-year escalation over the past twenty years of the average grade of students at Cornell University, one of our finest Ivy League colleges. Over the past few years, the same complaints of grade inflation have routinely been made by faculty and administrators at Harvard, Princeton, and a host of other top-flight universities.

In organizations, things are not that different. HR managers frequently complain about the fact that performance appraisal ratings are notoriously inflated and that people simply aren't being told the truth about just how well they're doing. There's probably no veteran HR professional who hasn't had the distasteful experience of talking to a line manager who has finally made the decision to fire a marginal performer after years of shoddy work, only to discover that the individual has a drawerful of performance appraisals in his file, all with stellar ratings.

This book will help solve this common problem. Certainly one reason that managers don't give their subordinates honest, tough-minded appraisals of their performance is that they simply lack the courage to provide straight-between-the-eyes feedback, and no book will cure this sad situation. But a more important reason for the problem of organizational grade inflation that occurs in so many companies is that managers have never been told exactly how to set specific goals. They don't know how to communicate exactly what results they're looking for and how the subordinate's performance will be measured. No one has shown them how to work with subordinates to identify their strengths and weaknesses. They don't have the skills they need to conduct an effective performance assessment or explain to a member of the team precisely where her performance needs to be improved. They would do the right thing if someone would just show them how, but they've been left to figure it out on their own. So they muddle through as best they can and take the path of least resistance.

This book represents an important step toward curing this common problem. Managers and those on their team should look at the performance appraisal process as a real opportunity to clarify expectations and thereby remove much of the mystery that surrounds performance appraisal. A recent survey conducted by the Corporate Leadership Council indicated that only 43 percent of all employees surveyed agreed with the statement "In my last performance appraisal I understood the standards I was being evaluated on." If people don't know how they're being evaluated, of course the performance appraisal process will generate feelings of anxiety and concerns about fairness. But if the manager clearly communicates her expectations, explains how performance will be measured, provides coaching throughout the year, assesses the quality of the individual's contributions objectively, and conducts a well-planned, professional appraisal interview, performance appraisal can be one of the most powerful team-building tools in the managerial arsenal.

Performance appraisal is too often seen as exclusively the manager's responsibility, with the employee being merely the target or the victim of the process. But, as Don Kirkpatrick makes clear in this book, performance management is not a unilateral process. Both the manager and the individual have responsibilities. When the need for performance improvement arises, the manager has the responsibility to spell out not just what needs to change but also what the manager will do to help the subordinate improve. The book provides a practical and straightforward model of a coaching plan that shows managers how to help their people be successful.

Don Kirkpatrick has distilled almost fifty years of both practical and academic experience into a book that will be useful to managers, trainers, and HR professionals alike. He has provided insights from famous coaches to help managers meet their day-to-day coaching responsibilities. He has provided real-world examples that actually work and illustrations that make difficult concepts clear. He has shared the experiences of top-flight organizations and made available their forms and procedures so that every reader can immediately benefit from the lessons they have learned.

In his original foreword to the first edition of this valuable book, James L. Hayes, former CEO of the American Management Association, wrote, "There are some ideas in management whose time comes and goes and comes again, depending on circumstances of economy or fashion. There are other ideas whose time is ever present and whose demands for effective practice are immutable. Of these perhaps the most pertinent for all managers is the need for effective performance appraisal.'' In this book Don Kirkpatrick helps everyone concerned with human performance on the job excel in this challenging arena.

—Dick Grote

Chairman and CEO, Grote Consulting Corporation, Dallas, Texas

Author, *Discipline Without Punishment,*

The Complete Guide to Performance Appraisal, and

The Performance Appraisal Question and Answer Book

Preface

I f you are a manager who conducts performance appraisals with employees, you may find this book somewhat frustrating because you are probably locked into a program with forms and procedures. However, regardless of the forms and approaches you are required to use, you will find some practical help in such areas as clarifying what's expected, appraising performance, self-appraisal, conducting the appraisal interview, developing a performance improvement plan, and on-the-job coaching. You'll be particularly interested in the comments from some nationally known athletic coaches, and you'll be amazed by how much of their advice will apply directly to you on your job.

This book includes two case studies; philosophy, principles, and approaches from various organizations; and sample forms. This material will be of practical use as you evaluate your own philosophy, forms, and procedures.

Also, this book may help you discover why your program isn't working as well as you'd like it to. If you have any suggestions that you think will help improve your performance review program, pass them along to those in your organization who are responsible for the program's administration.

If you have an overall responsibility for an effective performance appraisal and review program in your organization, this book will have special benefit for you. If you already have a program, you can compare it to the ideas, examples, and case studies presented here. Of particular interest and benefit to you will be Chapter 6, which describes the five requirements for effective programs and gives some specific ideas for improving them.

If you have no performance appraisal program at all or one that is not working out, this book will be of special interest and benefit. Study the principles and techniques described. Also, read the case study and "Notes from the Field" for ideas you can use or adapt. Finally, develop and implement your own program as described in Chapter 6.

The whole purpose of the book is to describe a practical program of appraisal and coaching that will help improve the performance of your employees. Good luck in reaching this objective.

—Donald L. Kirkpatrick

Acknowledgments

have many people to thank for making the book practical. They have contributed concepts, principles, and techniques that can be used and/or adapted to the performance appraisal programs of the readers. Those who contributed include Dick Grote (author of several books on performance appraisal), who wrote the Foreword; the many coaches who described the characteristics of an effective coach; Dianna Anderson and Merrill Anderson, who wrote the excellent chapter on coaching; Judith P. Clarke, who wrote the enlightening case study in the chapter on evaluating a training course on performance appraisal and coaching; Jeanne Armentrout and Cheryl Bennett, who wrote the detailed chapter covering both performance appraisal and coaching; the authors of "Notes from the Field," including Carolyn Henning, Stephen Glen, Dana Patrick, Carlyn Houston, Holly Burkett, my daughter Susan Muehlbach, Cathy Bolger, and Rita Laitres.

I also want to thank Adrienne Hickey, Barry Richardson, and Mike Sivilli of AMACOM for their encouragement and help.

Finally, I want to thank my wife, Fern, for her patience and understanding during the many hours I spent on the book.

IMPROVING

EMPLOYEE
PERFORMANCE

THROUGH

APPRAISAL

AND COACHING

Second Edition

A Conceptual Framework for the Appraisal/Coaching Process

n order to get improved performance from appraisal and coaching, a continuous process is necessary. It can be illustrated by the following diagram.

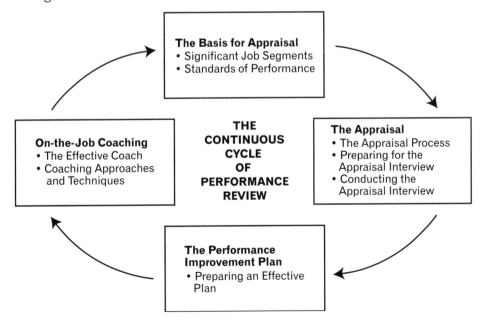

The Basis for Appraisal
• Significant Job Segments
• Standards of Performance

On-the-Job Coaching
• The Effective Coach
• Coaching Approaches and Techniques

THE CONTINUOUS CYCLE OF PERFORMANCE REVIEW

The Appraisal
• The Appraisal Process
• Preparing for the Appraisal Interview
• Conducting the Appraisal Interview

The Performance Improvement Plan
• Preparing an Effective Plan

The first step is to clarify what's expected of the employee. This can be done by identifying significant job segments and developing standards of performance. The second step is to appraise performance and to discuss it in an appraisal interview. At the conclusion of the interview, a performance improvement plan can be developed. On-the-job coaching is necessary to help the employee improve his performance. The first step is repeated on whatever time schedule is established by the organization.

The pretest that follows presents the philosophy and principles discussed in this book. Complete it to see what you believe before you begin to read. The same test is included on page 112 as a posttest to complete *after* you read that far in this book. My suggested answers, and the reasons for them, follow the posttest. I suggest that you not look at the answers until after you have finished both tests. Then you can compare your two scores to see what you have learned.

Pretest

Write "yes" in front of each statement if you agree and "no" if you disagree.

_____   1. Every employee has responsibility for his own development.
_____   2. Every manager has responsibility for the growth and development of all employees.
_____   3. Every organization has responsibility for the growth and development of all employees.
_____   4. Most people want to know how they are doing their job as the manager sees it.
_____   5. Most employees would like to improve their performance.
_____   6. Less than maximum performance of an employee is often due to factors over which the employee has no control.
_____   7. The same performance review program (forms, procedures, interview) should be used both for improved performance and for salary administration.
_____   8. Performance appraisals and reviews should be voluntary on the part of managers.
_____   9. The more writing required of the manager on the appraisal form, the more effective the program.
_____ 10. The less paperwork required in a performance appraisal program, the more effective the program.
_____ 11. Appraisal forms should include about a 50-50 balance be-

tween items dealing with performance and those dealing with personality.

_____ 12. Agreement on significant job segments and standards of performance is an important prerequisite to the appraisal of job performance.

_____ 13. The word "appraisal" connotes both judgment and communication.

_____ 14. A group appraisal of a person's performance is better than having an appraisal just by the manager.

_____ 15. A self-appraisal by the employee is a good idea.

_____ 16. The main objective of the appraisal interview is for the manager to explain and sell her prepared appraisal to the employee.

_____ 17. In the interview discussing the performance of the employee, there should be no surprises.

_____ 18. In an appraisal interview, it's a good idea to have at least three people present (for example, the manager, the employee, and a neutral party, such as a representative of the human resources department).

_____ 19. Appraisal interviews should be a pleasant experience for both manager and employee.

_____ 20. In the appraisal interview, the manager should not show his completed form to the employee.

_____ 21. An organization can be assured that an effective appraisal interview has been conducted if the employee is required to sign the form.

_____ 22. In an appraisal interview, the manager should always give her appraisal of the employee and then ask the employee for reactions and comments.

_____ 23. It's a good idea to divide the appraisal interview into two or three separate interviews.

_____ 24. An appraisal interview should always end on a positive note.

_____ 25. A specific written performance improvement plan is an important part of a performance review program.

_____ 26. A performance improvement plan should include what should be done, by whom, and when.

_____ 27. It's a good idea for employees to work toward performance improvement in several areas at once.

_____ 28. Coaching means the same as counseling.

_____ 29. Coaching a group of employees is similar to coaching a team of athletes.

_____ 30. On-the-job coaching is necessary to be sure that the performance improvement plan is implemented.

_____ 31. Coaching on the job should include praise for good work, as well as constructive criticism and help to improve poor work.

_____ 32. Improvement in performance should be immediately rewarded by the manager.

_____ 33. Rewards should be based on performance, rather than seniority.

_____ 34. Both the manager and the employee should have a copy of all completed forms.

_____ 35. A copy of the completed appraisal forms should be put in the personnel file of the employee.

_____ 36. A standard of performance should be:

_____   a. Established for a job.

_____   b. Established for an individual.

_____   c. An "acceptable" level of performance.

_____   d. A "well done" level of performance.

_____   e. Challenging (requires stretch but can be reached).

_____   f. Unattainable (requires stretch and can't be reached).

_____   g. Agreed on between manager and employee.

_____   h. Determined solely by the manager.

_____   i. Determined solely by the employee.

_____   j. Jointly determined by manager and employee.

_____   k. Clear to manager and employee.

_____   l. Written.

_____   m. Time oriented.

_____   n. Specific (numbers, percentages, dollars, wherever possible).

_____   o. The basis for performance appraisal.

_____   p. Subject to change.

_____ 37. The same appraisal forms and procedures can be effectively used by any kind of organization.

_____ 38. The people who supervise a performance appraisal program must do more than simply oversee paperwork. They must communicate the program and sell it to those involved.

_____ 39. It takes no real training to conduct performance reviews effectively.

_____ 40. Administrative controls must be established for performance review programs.

Introduction and Overview

How to Get Maximum Performance from Employees

The major challenge that faces managers in all types of organizations is how to get maximum performance from their employees. First, they need to motivate their employees to get maximum effort from them. This means ensuring that people will try their best to do the job; whether the manager's effort is successful can be measured by the energy and time employees expend. If only motivation guaranteed maximum results! Unfortunately, much of this energy and time is wasted. Therefore, the second requirement is for managers to get maximum accomplishments and achievements from their employees. This two-fold challenge—effort plus results—faces every manager.

Ways to Improve Employee Performance

On a recent visit to India, I was asked by the manager of a small clothing shop in the Chola Hotel in Madras, "What is the one thing that managers can do to get their employees to do their best?" I replied that it isn't as simple as "just one thing." He repeated the question: "What is the *one thing* that managers can do to get their employees to do their best?" I hemmed and hawed and started to tell him that there are eight things.

He interrupted and said, "Don't tell me eight, tell me *one!*" I said, "I can't." He replied, "Then I'll tell you!" I answered, "O.K., you tell me."

And he did. "You have to give your people encouragement. It doesn't mean just money, although that's one of the ways to encourage your people. It also means a pat on the back when they do a good job. If you rub them into the ground with your heel, you won't get the best work from them, and they won't like you, besides."

I was supposed to be the expert who was conducting seminars on leadership for managers in business and government in India. And I received a good lesson in motivation from a shopkeeper in the basement of a hotel.

It isn't quite as simple as encouragement, but that's a good start. Here are the eight conditions I was going to describe to the shop owner that will get maximum effort and results from employees:

1. Make the job important in the eyes of the employee.
2. Select a person who has the potential to perform the job.
3. Clarify what's expected of the employee in the job.
4. Train the employee in the necessary knowledge, skills, and attitudes.
5. Evaluate performance, and communicate results and expectations to the employee.
6. Help him improve performance.
7. Build and maintain rapport with the employee.
8. Reward for performance.

These eight conditions are developed further in the following paragraphs.

Make the job important. People who feel their jobs are important are more apt to try their best, because they realize that it does make a difference how well the job is done. When the manager increases the scope and importance of the job, people are more apt to put forth maximum effort.

Select the right person. The well-known Peter Principle states that people tend to rise to their level of incompetence.[1] One reason for incompetence is that people are promoted on the basis of performance. Where the old job and the new ones are alike, performance is a valid basis for promotion. But where the jobs are different, performance may be a poor criterion for promotion. This is especially true where the promotion is from "doing" to management. Management, according to Lawrence A. Appley, past president of the American Management Associations, is "getting things done through others," rather than doing them yourself.

When you are considering a person for a job, whether it is an entry-level job or a promotion, the problem is to match the person to the job. Usually the match is not a perfect one because the candidates have never done that exact job before. Therefore, *the potential* of the person must be determined. In other words, you should ask: "With the proper training, would this person be able to perform the job successfully?"

Potential is a difficult thing to measure. Typically, the candidates' backgrounds are analyzed with special emphasis on education and experience. Next, interviews are conducted, and the candidates are evaluated on the basis of their answers to questions, as well as their appearance and the impression they make on the interviewer. Often references are checked to find out from former supervisors or acquaintances how the people performed in previous jobs. Some organizations also use testing and assessment centers. The higher the job level, the more time and money an organization should spend to determine potential.

There is good evidence that many people are promoted to supervisory positions who never should have been. The typical selection process places undue emphasis on performance, years of service, and cooperative attitude. A more systematic approach stresses the importance of desire—*wanting* to be a supervisor—as well as leadership qualities.

Clarify what's expected. Many frustrations and failures occur because employees don't understand exactly what's expected of them by their supervisors. They put forth much effort doing what they *think* is wanted, rather than what *is* wanted.

When I worked for a large chemical corporation, my friend Ken worked for Michelle, a vice president. One day Ken and I had this conversation:

Ken: I think I'm in trouble with Michelle, my supervisor.
Don: What do you mean?
Ken: I don't think Michelle is happy with my performance.

Don: What makes you think so?

Ken: I just have a feeling.

Don: Has she told you she's unhappy with your performance?

Ken: No, she hasn't told me anything about my performance since I started working here nine months ago.

Don: Then why do you think she's unhappy?

Ken: Well, she gave me a three-page job description when I came, and I can't do everything that she expects.

Don: What are you doing?

Ken: I'm doing the things I think are most important.

Don: And?

Ken: I'm not sure *she* thinks they are the most important.

Don: I have a suggestion.

Ken: What?

Don: Go and see Michelle and tell her your problem. Take the job description with you, and show her the things you are doing and the things you aren't doing. And see if she agrees.

Ken: I can't.

Don: Why not?

Ken: Because she's not available. She's either up in the president's office or else she's out of town or busy entertaining some important people.

Don: Then the only suggestion I have for you is to try to do the things that *she* thinks are important instead of those *you* think are important.

About three months later, I learned that Ken had been terminated for "poor performance." Because of our conversation, I was most interested in learning more about the termination. I got my chance one noon when I saw Michelle sitting alone in the company dining room.

Don: Michelle, can I talk with you for a few minutes?

Michelle: Sure.

Don: I understand that you terminated Ken a couple of week ago.

Michelle: That's right.

Don: Would you mind telling me why?

Michelle: Not at all. He just wasn't doing his job.

Don: Can you be more specific?

Michelle: Sure. He was spending his time and energy on the unim-

portant parts of his job and wasn't getting the most important
things done.

Don: Did you ever tell him what the most important parts of his job
were?

Michelle: I gave him a job description. I expected him to be smart
enough to know which things were most important!

Then I related to Michelle the conversation that Ken and I had had
several months earlier. Michelle replied, "Well, that's life. If he wasn't
smart enough to separate the important things from the unimportant
things, that's his problem!"

I was very disappointed in Michelle, not so much for actually termi-
nating Ken but for her attitude about it. I had hoped that Michelle was
feeling some guilt and might have learned something from the incident.

There are many Michelles in management who do not clarify what
is expected of employees. And there are many Kens who suffer the consequences even if they have the necessary qualifications and try their
best. I only hope that most of the Michelles who read this book will
look at their own situations and either take the initiative in clarifying
what's expected or at least make themselves available to employees
who have the courage to ask for clarification themselves.

Train the person. No matter how well the person matches the job,
some training is always necessary. Training includes the teaching of
knowledge, skills, and attitudes. The first step is to decide who will be
the trainer. The qualifications are:

Knowledge and skill in doing the job
A desire to teach
Communication skills
Patience
A positive attitude toward the organization and the job to be
learned
A knowledge of teaching methods and procedures
Time to train

Many supervisors like to do the training personally. They are usually the best ones if they meet the other requirements listed above. But
some are too busy or lack one or more of the qualifications, so they
delegate the training to someone else. If this is done, the supervisor

should be sure that the chosen trainer is qualified; even then, some checking is necessary to be sure that an effective job has been done. The supervisor may delegate the task to another person, but the supervisor has final responsibility and must live with the results.

If the person being trained is a supervisor, the training should emphasize management knowledge, skills, and attitudes. This means that the manager usually has to call on outside help for the training, such as in-house management courses or those presented by outside organizations. And it's a good idea to begin the management training as soon as the new supervisor is appointed. As an example, a one-day conference at the Management Institute of the University of Wisconsin— Extension is called "Basics of Management for New Supervisors," and it is designed for organizations that do not have a similar in-house program. Other universities, associations, and consultants offer similar training programs.

In addition to courses, a management library should be available for new supervisors. The books should be carefully selected so that they are readable and practical for the supervisor.

The jump from "doer" to manager is a big one. Great care must be taken to ensure that the new supervisor not only knows the difference between a "doer" and a manager but also has the knowledge, skills, and attitudes necessary for success.

Evaluate performance and communicate the appraisal. People want to know how they are doing on the job, and it is the responsibility of the manager to tell them. This requires the manager to evaluate their performance and communicate the appraisal to them. This process of appraisal and communication should be regular and ongoing; managers should not wait until the annual appraisal interview to do it. Nor should they rely entirely on informal day-to-day coaching. Instead, both formal and informal appraisals are necessary. This book covers in detail the process as well as the forms and procedures for an effective performance appraisal program.

Help the person improve. The appraisal should measure how well the various parts of the job are being performed. It should identify the employee's strengths, as well as the aspects of the job where improved performance is needed. When these have been identified and agreed on between manager and employee, a performance improvement plan should be developed and implemented. Methods for doing this are covered in detail in this book.

Build and maintain rapport. Rapport can be defined as a good working relationship or a climate of mutual trust and respect between manager and employee. To build rapport, the manager must try to understand and meet the employee's needs and wants, not just the organization's. Only when both are met has the manager really succeeded.

There are many ways to build rapport. An obvious one is for the manager to praise good work and give credit when due. Another is for the manager to take a personal interest in the hobbies, family, problems, and other things that are dear to the heart of the employee. Perhaps the most important thing that a manager can do is to make clear that he or she is interested in the successful performance of the employee on the present job. Also, the manager must show an interest in the future of the employee with the organization.

This consideration for the future presents a real challenge to a manager. Many organizations have developed formal approaches to career planning and development. They have found there are some advantages and some drawbacks to the formal approach. On the positive side, it demonstrates a concerted effort to see that employees move ahead in a systematic fashion. It shows that the organization is willing to spend time and money to be sure that promotions are made fairly. On the negative side, employees might get the impression that the promotions are going to come in a planned progression. The organization might give false hopes to those who aren't going to be promoted or to those whose promotion opportunity is far in the future.

Advancement in an organization usually depends on three separate and distinct factors:

1. The interests, desires, and aspirations of the employee
2. The potential of the employee as determined by management
3. Openings

Some organizations ask employees to indicate their ambitions and goals. Sometimes this is done formally at the conclusion of a performance appraisal interview. Sometimes it is done informally in conversations between manager and employee. And some organizations do it as a separate project by sending forms for employees to complete. All these approaches can be effective in gathering this important information.

In addition to determining the interests, aspirations, ambitions, and goals of employees, management must determine potential for advancement. At best, the process requires some subjectivity and comes down to an educated guess. The attitudes of many unions, for example, is that you can't really tell whether a person can perform a higher-level job unless you give the person a chance to try. And in some cases they may be right. But management must determine potential with as much objectivity as possible. The assessment center approach is one of the best ways.

The final factor that determines advancement is the number of promotional opportunities that will occur. In most organizations, large and small, people can't advance unless an opening is created by retirement, promotion, death, transfer, resignation, or growth. In some organizations, these openings occur frequently. In others, they occur infrequently.

Career planning and development must consider all three of these factors. There are eight possible combinations of these three factors that a manager could face. In the examples, the term "management" is used to mean whoever inside or outside the organization assesses potential.

> Situation 1: Kimberly wants to be promoted, management doesn't feel she has the potential to do a higher-level job, and a promotional opportunity exists.
>
> Situation 2: Kevin wants to be promoted, management feels he is promotable, but no openings exist.
>
> Situation 3: Kathy has no desire to be promoted, management feels she has the potential for promotion, and no openings exist.
>
> Situation 4: Barbara has no desire to be promoted, management feels she has the potential, and an opening exists.
>
> Situation 5: Neil wants to be promoted, management feels he has the potential, and an opening exists.
>
> Situation 6: Chris has no desire to be promoted, management feels he has no potential, and no openings exist.
>
> Situation 7: Colleen has a desire to be promoted, management doesn't feel she's promotable, and no openings exist.
>
> Situation 8: Bryan has no desire to be promoted, management doesn't feel he's promotable, and an opening exists.

These situations can be depicted in a table, as shown below. Quick reference to the table shows that situations 6 (Chris) and 8 (Bryan) are easy to handle. In both cases, the desire of the employee agrees with

	Desire for Promotion	Potential for Promotion	Openings
1. Kimberly	Yes	No	Yes
2. Kevin	Yes	Yes	No
3. Kathy	No	Yes	No
4. Barbara	No	Yes	Yes
5. Neil	Yes	Yes	Yes
6. Chris	No	No	No
7. Colleen	Yes	No	No
8. Bryan	No	No	Yes

the analysis of potential by management. Neither Chris nor Bryan wants to be promoted, so no problem exists.

At first glance, situation 5 (Neil) also seems to be an easy one. Neil wants to be promoted, management feels he can handle the job, and an opening exists. However, complications arise because Neil is a white male. Situation 1 (Kimberly) must also be considered. Even though management doesn't think she has the potential, she wants the job. And potential is subject to debate. Besides, upgrading minorities may be part of management's obligation under its affirmative action program.

Also, situation 4 (Barbara) must be considered when we consider Neil and Kimberly. Management has stamped her promotable even though she has no desire to be promoted. Perhaps she doesn't realize that she can do the job or hasn't really thought too much about it. Isn't it the obligation of management—as well as a sign of good judgment—to persuade her that she can handle the job? So now the organization has three people to consider in filling the opening.

Situation 2 (Kevin) presents an interesting challenge to management. Kevin wants to be promoted and is considered qualified, but no openings exist. Can you keep him, or will he become impatient and leave? Possible approaches for keeping him include job enrichment, special assignments, delegated tasks, and other types of challenges and rewards that might satisfy him until an opening occurs.

Situation 7 (Colleen) presents another challenge to management. Colleen wants to be promoted, but management doesn't feel she has the potential to be successful. No immediate problem exists because there are no openings. But as soon as an opening occurs, the organization will have the same problem it currently has with situation 1 (Kimberly).

Situation 3 (Kathy) offers a pleasant problem for management with no particular time pressures. Kathy has no desire to move up, but management feels she has potential. This allows management time to persuade her that she is promotable or to wait until an opening occurs and treat her case like situation 4 (Barbara).

These eight situations illustrate the problems of career planning and development. The planning must be less than scientific, and plans must be flexible instead of firm. Goals and aspirations as well as potential should be frankly discussed. Also, the existence or possibility of openings should be made clear. Conversations should result in a realistic understanding of the employee's future in the organization, and the entire process should demonstrate clearly that the manager is sincerely interested in the employee and his or her future success and happiness. These conversations can help to develop rapport between manager and employee and help achieve maximum effort and performance.

As stated earlier, many organizations have formalized their approach to career planning and development. An example is the Crocker National Bank of California.[2] During the first two and a half years of the program, more than 200 employees were involved, ranging from senior vice presidents to bank tellers, with a majority in lower exempt professional positions. In San Francisco, Los Angeles, and San Diego, the program was made available to any of the 14,000 employees whose supervisors or employee relations representatives recommended them. The following steps were taken in developing the program:

1. Obtained the support, cooperation, and participation of senior management.
2. Integrated career counseling into the performance appraisal system.
3. Obtained adequate professional staff to initiate a system for career counseling.
4. Developed a communications network of resource people and a centralized job information and education resource center.
5. Established clear referral procedures for career counseling.
6. Initiated individual career counseling services.
   a. Counseled employees on self-analysis, diagnosis of the organization, and action plans.
   b. Educated managers in career planning techniques and the bank's career opportunities.
7. Evaluated the program every six months.
8. Reviewed progress of counseled employees every six months.

9. Updated information files regularly.
10. Planned and presented career planning workshops on a pilot basis.
11. Trained and certified employee relations representatives in career counseling techniques and knowledge of the bank.
12. Presented career planning workshops on a continual basis.

An extensive research project was implemented to evaluate the career counseling program. Here are one-year results for 1978:

Turnover was reduced by 65 percent.
Performance was improved by 85 percent.
Promotability was increased by 75 percent.
Savings of $1,950,000 were realized.

Reward for performance. The eighth and final requirement for getting maximum effort and performance from employees is to reward for performance, not on the basis of years of service, favoritism, or anything else. Rewards can be monetary, such as wage incentives, merit salary increases, bonuses, profit sharing, and prizes. Or they can be nonmonetary, such as praise, special job assignments, more responsibility, delegated tasks, asking for ideas, better working conditions, status symbols, and authority.

Probably the most effective and least recognized of the nonmonetary rewards is authority, or freedom to act. There are four degrees of authority:

1. Do what the supervisor says—no more and no less.
2. Suggest and recommend to the supervisor, but take no action until the manager approves.
3. Act, but tell the supervisor afterward.
4. Act.

In the first two degrees, the employee has been given no authority. The second degree is more pleasant than the first, but there is no freedom to act until the supervisor says O.K.

The third and fourth degrees give the employee the authority to act. In the third, the supervisor wants to know about the action after it has been done. There are several reasons why this may be. Many supervisors want to know what goes on in their departments, either because they feel they should know or because their managers expect them to know. Also, if the action causes problems, the supervisor should know so that corrective action can be taken and future problems avoided.

There is also a different kind of reason for knowing what action the employee has taken, one related to rewards for performance. If the employee consistently makes poor decisions, the supervisor should move the employee back to degree 2, in which the employee checks with the supervisor *before* action is taken. If the action in degree 3 is consistently good, the employee can be moved to degree 4. In other words, performance is rewarded with more authority. And this type of reward is very significant to many people.

Promotion has not been mentioned as a reward. Obviously, past performance should be considered when a person is a candidate for promotion. Where the new job is entirely different from the present job, performance should carry very little weight. As was stated earlier, this is especially true when a person is promoted from a "doer" to a position as a first-line supervisor. If the new job is similar to the present job, performance should carry much more weight as one of the criteria for selection. For example, when a person is promoted from one level of management to another, promotion is an important reward for performance.

Summary

Managers must depend on the performance of their employees. As one manager put it, "When they're doing their jobs, I'm doing mine!" This section has described the eight requirements for getting maximum effort and performance from employees. The rest of the book deals in detail with three of these eight factors: clarifying what's expected, appraising and communicating quality of performance, and coaching for improved performance. It is important to put these three factors in the proper context and to recognize that other things can also be done to improve performance.

The Performance Review Program

Before we go any further, let's define some important terms that are used throughout the book. Then four aspects of a performance review program are discussed in detail: program objectives, forms and procedures, frequency of reviews, and equal employment opportunity and affirmative action considerations.

Definition of Terms

The term "performance review" is used in this book to include significant job segments, standards of performance, appraisal, appraisal interview, and on-the-job coaching. These terms are used with the following meanings:

Significant Job Segments. These are the most important parts of the job. Not every detailed duty and responsibility should be evaluated. The word "significant" is a subjective term, and each organization (and even each manager) should determine its exact meaning. Chapter 2 covers this.

Standards of Performance. These are the conditions that exist when the work has been done in an acceptable manner. They explain *how well* the job should be done, while significant job segments describe *what* should be done. These standards become the basis on which performance is judged, and are discussed in Chapter 2, as well.

Appraisal. This is the evaluation or judgment of how well the job has been done. It is always done by the supervisor with or without input from other people.

A self-appraisal is an evaluation by the employee. Some organizations require it in their performance review programs. Other organizations do not include it or leave it up to the supervisor whether to ask the employee for a self-appraisal. Chapter 3 deals with this.

Appraisal Interview. The appraisal interview is the discussion of the appraisal between the supervisor (reviewer) and the employee (person being reviewed). As described in this book, it consists of the following aspects:

Communication of the supervisor's appraisal to the employee
Communication of the employee's appraisal to the supervisor
Agreement on a fair appraisal
Agreement on the strengths of the employee
Agreement on the job segments needing improvement
Agreement on a performance improvement plan that spells out the
    specific things to be done to improve performance

The length of interview time to cover all these items varies greatly. In most cases, the supervisor should conduct two or even three interviews instead of trying to discuss all of them in one interview. Chapter 3 covers the appraisal interview, and Chapter 4 discusses the performance improvement plan.

On-the-Job Coaching. After the formal performance appraisal interview has been conducted, both the supervisor and the employee go back to their day-to-day activities. Part of the supervisor's activity should be the on-the-job coaching of the employee. This coaching should be a direct follow-up to be sure the agreed-on performance improvement plan is carried out. It should serve as a regular means for praising good performance and correcting mistakes. It should be the vehicle for updating significant job segments and standards of performance. In short, it should be a method for following up on an interview and avoiding surprises in the next formal performance appraisal interview. Chapter 5 covers coaching.

Program Objectives

There are three basic reasons why organizations have performance appraisal programs: to provide information for salary administration, to provide information for promotion, and to improve performance on the present job. The next three subsections deal with each of these objectives and its relationship to performance appraisal.

To Provide Information for Salary Administration. Many factors should be considered in determining salary increases. They include:

1. The employee's performance. This can be measured by actual results or by results compared to objectives if the organization has a program of management by objectives.
2. The amount of improvement in performance since the last salary increase.
3. The minimum and maximum salary range for the job and where the employee's salary is presently located in the range.
4. A comparison of the employee's performance with the performance of others doing the same or similar jobs.
5. A comparison of the employee's salary with salaries of others doing the same or similar jobs.
6. Length of service. Some increase is usually given for being on the job another year.
7. Education. In some organizations, additional education, particularly if a degree is granted, is rewarded with a salary increase.
8. The rate of inflation since the last salary increase. A raise given for this reason is usually called a cost-of-living increase.
9. Established guidelines. These could be established by outside

sources, such as the president of the United States, or by company policy. For example, a maximum salary increase amount can be set.

10. The salary that other organizations are paying people in the same or similar jobs.

Performance appraisal systems can provide information relating to factors 1, 2, and 4. It is important to recognize that many other factors must also be considered in determining salary adjustments.

To Provide Information for Promotion. Many performance review programs include the appraisal of potential, as well as of performance. Usually, the manager considers past performance as one indication of the potential of the individual to do higher-level jobs. Past performance is probably the best predictor of future performance if the present job and the future job are pretty much the same. Other factors to be considered are desire, intelligence, personality, emotional stability, leadership skills, and other characteristics related to the job to be filled. An individual may be an outstanding performer and not be promotable because the requirements for success on the present job are different from those for the higher-level job. Likewise, an employee can be performing a job at a mediocre or even unsatisfactory level and be promotable because the necessary knowledge and skills are entirely different.

To Improve Performance on the Present Job. The third objective of performance review is to improve performance on the present job. To achieve this, past performance is reviewed, and steps are taken to improve future performance. This book provides philosophy, principles, approaches, and specific forms and techniques for accomplishing this objective.

One Program for All Three Objectives?

Some organizations have one program that is designed to accomplish all three objectives. Usually such programs fail to accomplish the third one, which is to improve performance on the present job. The main reason is that there is so much emotion involved in the discussion of salary and promotion that it is not possible to be objective about ways to improve performance. For example, a person may be doing an outstanding job, have substantially improved performance since the last review, and still not receive a large salary increase. Also, a person may be an outstanding performer and yet be deemed not promotable. These situations don't lend themselves to encouraging and helping employees improve their performance.

Table 1-1 reveals a number of significant differences between performance reviews for improved performance and those for salary administration purposes. Because of these differences, performance review for improved performance should be separated from performance review for determination and discussion of salary increase and promotability.

In an extensive study on performance reviews, researchers at General Electric came to the following conclusion:

Implicit in performance appraisal programs as now structured are two distinct objectives: (1) letting a person know where he or she stands via ratings and salary actions, and (2) motivating him or her to improve. The results of this study showed that attempts to achieve the first objective frequently produce threat and defensiveness, and these reactions, in turn, interfere with the achievement of the second objective.

A merit-pay type of salary plan makes some variety of summary judgment or rating of performance necessary, or at least desirable; but this rating should *not* be expected to serve also as a primary medium for changing performance. Quite separate from this rating activity, the manager can use goal planning discussions, special assignments, and other techniques to achieve improved performance on the part of employees.[3]

Table 1-1. Comparison of two kinds of performance reviews.

	Performance Reviews for Salary Administration	Performance Reviews for Improved Performance
Looking	Backward	Forward
Considering	Overall performance	Detailed performance
Comparing with	Other people	Job standards and objectives
Determined by	Manager, higher management, human resources department	Manager and employee together
Interview climate	Subjective, emotional	Objective, unemotional
Factors to consider	Salary range, total money available, inflation, seniority, performance, education	Performance

Clearly, then, the two kinds of performance reviews should be separate. One approach is to have separate annual reviews for salary administration and for improved performance, scheduled approximately six months apart.

Forms and Procedures

Many different types of performance review forms have been developed and used by organizations. They vary all the way from a blank piece of paper to a twenty-two-page form used by a general sales manager for five regional sales managers. Some forms are very simple with a list of factors to be rated and a few boxes to check. Others require the manager to work with the employee to develop the factors on which the appraisal will be based. There is no right or wrong form. The important thing is that the form accomplish the objectives of the program.

To achieve improved job performance, a form should be designed to accomplish this objective and not necessarily to accomplish the objectives of determining salary increases or potential for promotion. If the form provides information that is helpful in determining potential or salary increases, so much the better.

In addition to accomplishing program objectives, the form should fit the organization or department that is using it. For example, the form for appraising a production foreman may be quite different from one for an office supervisor or an engineer. Or one form may be designed to apply to all types of jobs.

Another consideration in designing a form is that it can be used effectively by the managers. For example, if an organization has limited clerical help, poor facilities in which to conduct interviews, and managers who hate paperwork, common sense tells us to keep it simple. On the other hand, if the managers are sophisticated and oriented to paperwork, a more complicated form can be used.

As nearly as possible, the form should be self-explanatory. A manager should not have to study a manual to understand how the form should be completed. Also, the words used should be as clear as possible. Words like "dependability," "responsibility," and even "quality" have different meanings to different people. The manager might think "quality, accurate work" means perfect work, or work with no scrap, while the employee might think it means work without too many mistakes or without too much scrap.

All forms should include not only what should be done but also how well it should be done. This combination clarifies what is expected so that the manager's and the employee's appraisals will be based on the same understanding of the job.

Examples of various types of forms are provided in Chapter 11. Comments are included on the positive and negative aspects of each form.

Frequency of Reviews

Formal performance reviews covering the entire job of an employee should be conducted at least once a year by the manager; twice a year is preferable. The frequency is influenced by five main factors:

1. *How complicated is the program?* If the forms and procedures are complicated and involve much time and paperwork, the review should be done only once a year. If they are relatively simple and take little time, it can be done semiannually.
2. *How enthusiastic are the managers about the program?* If managers are enthusiastic about reviewing performance and feel it helps both relationships and productivity, it can be done twice a year. If it becomes a chore they dread and complain about, once a year is probably sufficient. It is better to start on a once-a-year basis and move to twice a year than to start with twice-a-year reviews and have the managers become discouraged and sour on the program.
3. *How much staff help is available to coordinate the program?* A coordinator and secretarial help are required to keep up with forms, schedules, and other paperwork. If enough such staff help is available, then twice a year might be advisable.
4. *How many people are going to be appraised by the manager?* This is related to the first factor because it influences the total time needed for performance reviews. In general, the more people that must be reviewed, the less frequently reviews can be done.
5. *How skilled are the appraisers?* If a new program is being integrated, it is better to require a formal appraisal only once a year while the appraisers learn the approach. This doesn't put too much demand on the managers' time and gets the program off to a good start. As the managers become trained and effective in conducting the reviews, the frequency might be increased to semiannual reviews, depending on the four factors described above.

Equal Employment Opportunity and Affirmative Action Considerations

Contract compliance regulations have been developed by the Office of Federal Contract Compliance Programs (OFCCP) of the Department of Labor. It is the policy of most companies—large and small—to have employment and personnel policies that are nondiscriminatory with regard to race, creed, color, sex, religion, and age. Such policies determine practices in recruitment and hiring, promotion, pay, training, layoff and recall, and reviews of employee performance.

An affirmative action program is a set of specific, results-oriented procedures by which an employer makes a commitment to apply every effort, in good faith, toward equal employment opportunity. Procedures without effort to make them work are meaningless, and effort undirected by specific and meaningful procedures is inadequate.

An acceptable affirmative action plan must include an analysis of areas within which the employer is deficient in the employment of minority groups and women. It must also include goals and timetables to which the employer's good-faith efforts will be directed to correct the deficiencies. The employer does this to achieve prompt and full utilization of minorities and women at all levels and in all segments of the workforce where deficiencies may exist.

A formal affirmative action plan is implemented as follows:

1. The employer should validate worker specifications by division, department, location, or other organizational units and by job title, using job performance criteria.
2. All personnel involved in the recruitment, screening, selection, promotion, disciplinary, and related processes should be carefully selected and trained to ensure elimination of bias in all personnel actions.
3. The employer should ensure that minority and female employees are given equal opportunity for promotion. Suggestions for achieving this result include:
   (a) Develop and implement formal performance appraisal programs.
   (b) Establish valid requirements for promotion, directly related to the job. These should be used exclusively when deciding on promotions.
   (c) Review the qualifications of all employees to ensure that minorities and women are given full opportunities for transfers and promotions.

(d) Establish formal career counseling programs, including attitude development, education aid, job rotation, a buddy system, and similar programs.

(e) Provide full opportunity for minority and female employees. Encourage them to participate in all company-sponsored educational, training, recreational, and social activities, and provide them with the same benefits as other employees. Apply all personnel programs uniformly to all employees without exception.

(f) Evaluate the work performance of supervisors on the basis of their equal employment opportunity efforts and results, as well as other criteria.

Summary

This section first defined the various terms connected with performance review. Next, the three major objectives of a program were described. Emphasis was placed on the fact that different approaches must be used for the different objectives.

Forms and procedures were then discussed with guidelines for selecting the right ones for a particular organization. The section on frequency of reviews described the considerations in deciding whether to do them annually or semiannually. Finally, guidelines for equal employment opportunity and affirmative action programs were presented.

Notes

1. Laurence J. Peter and Raymond Hull, *The Peter Principle: Why Things Always Go Wrong* (New York: Bantam, 1970).

2. Karen R. Kobrosky, "Approach to Career Management." Copyright © Karen R. Kobrosky. Published by Crocker National Bank, San Francisco, 1979. All rights reserved.

3. E. Kay, J. P. French, Jr., and H. H. Meyer, "A Study of the Performance Appraisal Interview" (Lynn, Mass.: Behavioral Research Service at General Electric, 1962).

CHAPTER 2

The Basis for Appraisal

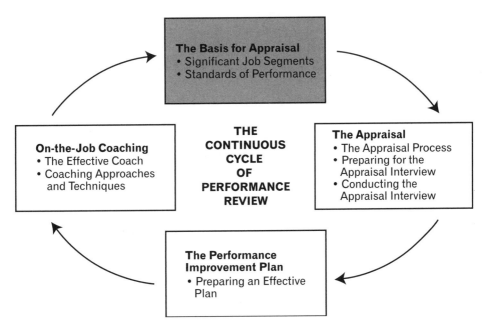

The Basis for Appraisal
• Significant Job Segments
• Standards of Performance

THE
CONTINUOUS
CYCLE
OF
PERFORMANCE
REVIEW

On-the-Job Coaching
• The Effective Coach
• Coaching Approaches
  and Techniques

The Appraisal
• The Appraisal Process
• Preparing for the
  Appraisal Interview
• Conducting the
  Appraisal Interview

The Performance
Improvement Plan
• Preparing an Effective
  Plan

n reading Dick Grote's *Performance Appraisal Question and Answer Book,* I was especially interested in his answer to this question: "Our performance appraisal form has a rating scale that asks whether the performance failed to meet expectations/met some expectations/met all expectations/exceeded expectations/and far exceeded expectations. If I haven't discussed my expectations with the employee, how do I rate performance?"

Here is his answer:

Contained in this question is the best argument for conducting a performance-planning discussion at the beginning of the year. If you don't know what you are looking for, how do you know when you find it?

Ideally the manager and the employee will discuss each of the manager's expectations at the start of the year and will come to an understanding of what the manager considers to be fully successful performance. If they do this, it will not only make it easier for the manager to accurately assess the quality of the job the individual has performed, it will also increase the probability that then two of them will agree on the accuracy of the assessment. But if no expectations have been set, then it's more difficult for the manager and more likely the two parties won't see eye to eye.

I agree with Dick on this very basic point—that a clear understanding of what is expected is essential. If there is no such understanding, the manager is likely to assess performance on the basis of what she expects of the employee, which may be very different from what the employee understood to be the job duties and responsibilities.

To avoid this problem, there are two requirements that must be met. The employee must understand both *what* is expected and *how well* the job is expected to be performed. I have called these two requirements "Significant Job Segments" and "Standards of Performance."

Significant Job Segments

The first step in the appraisal process is to select the significant segments of the job. Most organizations have job descriptions that cover the duties and responsibilities of jobs, and these can provide a good basis for selecting the significant job segments.

There is no hard-and-fast rule about the number of significant job segments to identify. It depends more on the wishes of the manager than it does on the nature of the job. Some managers consider nearly all aspects of an employee's job significant. Others prefer to select the four to six most significant aspects of the job. As a general rule, from six to eight segments are recommended.

Sample Lists of Significant Job Segments

Here are some actual examples taken from different types of organizations. They illustrate job descriptions and the significant job segments derived from them.

Position Title: ADMINISTRATIVE ASSISTANT

Duties and Responsibilities
- Composes general correspondence and reports using various software applications.
- Prepares graphs and charts for presentation materials.
- Gathers, compiles, and summarizes data.
- Enters and maintains spreadsheets.
- Arranges meetings, appointments, and conferences. Coordinates schedules, calendars, and conference calls. Makes travel arrangements.
- Establishes and maintains files.
- Responds and monitors telephone, voice mail, e-mail, and other correspondences as directed.
- Orders and maintains technical/desk equipment (i.e., phones, ergonomic equipment, desk set-ups) for new hires.
- Serves as a liaison between Inside Sales and other departments.
- Keeps time for area by maintaining vacation/absenteeism record and preparing payroll. Investigates and corrects any discrepancies associated with new hires or transfers.
- Handles confidential information, and maintains confidential files.
- Assumes other responsibilities as required or requested.

Significant Job Segments
- Composes general correspondence and reports.
- Prepares charts and graphs.
- Enters and maintains spreadsheets.
- Arranges meetings, appointments and conference calls.
- Establishes and maintains files.
- Orders and maintains technical desk equipment.
- Handles confidential information.

Position Title: SYSTEMS ANALYST

Duties and Responsibilities
- Researches and analyzes current systems.
- Analyzes current problems related to systems.

- Conducts meetings with users to determine problems and/or suggested improvements.
- Recommends equipment modifications or additions.
- Designs and develops new systems.
- Implements new or modified systems.
- Coordinates efforts with senior programmers and/or programmer analysts.
- Trains and develops assigned personnel in systems techniques.
- Serves as project leader.

Significant Job Segments
- Problem analysis
- Meetings with users
- Systems design
- Systems implementation
- Coordination with programmers
- Training and development of personnel
- Project leadership

Position Title: APPLICATION DEVELOPER, Information Technology

Duties and Responsibilities
- Designs, develops, tests, debugs, implements, documents, and maintains new applications, major new versions of existing applications, and enhancements to existing applications.
- Writes efficient code for the presentation (ASP.NET, HTML), business logic (components), and data (e.g., database SQL, stored procedures, triggers, functions) layers to create robust, flexible, scalable, highly available, low-maintenance, and cost-effective architecture. Core languages include Visual C#.net, JavaScript, and T-SQL.
- Utilizes standard development methodologies, coding standards, procedures, and techniques.
- Provides time estimates, progress status reports, problem reports, and reports on any issues pertaining to the projects to project managers, development leads, and architects in order to foster effective communication and coordination throughout the project life cycle.

- Works with architects and project managers to write, revise, and finalize user specifications, technical documentation, and other descriptive documentation that may support software applications (e.g., on-line help).
- Participates in periodic code reviews to ensure high quality and consistent coding practices.
- Adopts, follows, and contributes to the evolution of company standard best practices for application development and IT in general.
- Installs, tests, and maintains systems software, operating systems, compilers, and other systems.
- Participates in the development of training materials and/or on-line help materials for applications developed in-house.
- Acquires new knowledge through training programs and/or books/Web and keeps current with technologies.

Significant Job Segments
- Designs, develops, and tests new applications.
- Writes efficient codes for various applications.
- Uses standard development methodologies.
- Provides time estimates and various reports.
- Writes, revises, and finalizes descriptive documentation.
- Installs, tests, and maintains system software.

Position Title: SALES REPRESENTATIVE

Duties and Responsibilities
- Maintains current product, product application and capability, and product justification knowledge. Knows enough to be accepted and recognized as an expert in our field.
- Establishes friendly business and personal relationships with all potential customers for all assigned product lines in the assigned territory.
- Gets to know potential customers' organization and personnel. Knows intimately their responsibilities, products, economics, problems, requirements, methods, and so on.
- Conducts all activities in a manner contributory to maintenance of optimum corporate image, as defined in our sales and services policies.

- Organizes, plans, and schedules utilization of time to provide optimum effective account and territory coverage. Plans each specific sales call for most effective use of time.
- Creatively sells an optimum volume of all assigned products to all potential users in the assigned territory, commensurate with the potential for each product line.
- Conducts after-order follow-up in recognition of the fact that we are in a repeat business.
- Maintains knowledge of and adheres to company organizational procedures and policies regarding pricing, deliveries, warranty service, sales terms, forecasts, work hours, records, reports, vacation scheduling, use of company car, and so on.
- Identifies, keeps informed about, and reports on customers' present and future requirements, problems, and desires in order to facilitate our adapting our product lines and your efforts to these requirements.
- Keeps informed about and reports on all competitive products and developments.
- Utilizes home office assistance, advice, and guidance as required or offered.
- Cooperates with home office, other territories, and other sales and service personnel as required to accomplish overall sales objectives.
- Performs other specific assignments as required or requested.

Significant Job Segments
- Product knowledge
- Customer relations
- Customer knowledge
- Time utilization
- Sales volume
- Company knowledge
- Reports

Position Title: PAYROLL SUPERVISOR

Duties and Responsibilities
- Supervises the following:
  a. Compiling of data

    b. Tabulation of data

    c. Computing of detail

    d. Preparation of summaries and control figures

    e. Preparation of tax reports

- Assigns work to employees.
- Interviews, selects, and trains employees.
- Evaluates and counsels employees.
- Recommends people for promotion.
- Recommends salary increases.

Significant Job Segments

- Data compilation, tabulation, and computing
- Preparation of reports
- Work assignment
- Personnel
- Promotion and salary increases

Position Title: MACHINE SHOP SUPERVISOR

Duties and Responsibilities

- Plans and coordinates precision machining of standardized components involving diversified operations and machine setups.
- Interprets and directs compliance with the union contract and labor relations policies.
- Enforces compliance with administrative practices and procedures.
- Establishes budgets.
- Maintains surveillance to ensure timely production that meets quality standards.
- Keeps costs within established budget.
- Interviews, selects, trains, counsels, promotes, evaluates, and assigns work to nonsalaried personnel.
- Acts as liaison with other divisions.

Significant Job Segments

- Planning
- Union contract and policies
- Practices and procedures
- Budgets

- Schedules
- Quality
- Personnel

Position Title: MARKETING ANALYST

Duties and Responsibilities
- Conducts market surveys.
- Gathers data on business activity trends.
- Gathers data on economic conditions.
- Prepares data for analysis by computer.
- Monitors computer output.
- Prepares reports.
- Participates in development of new company sales programs.
- Assists in implementation of new or modified management information systems.

Significant Job Segments
- Market research
- Computer interface
- Reports
- Sales programs
- Systems

Position Title: HEAD NURSE

Duties and Responsibilities
TO PATIENTS
- Plans safe, economical, and efficient nursing care.
- Sees that quality patient care is given to each patient in accordance with quality standards.
- Formulates and utilizes patient care plan to assist in resolving patient problems.
- Acts as liaison among patient, physician, and family.

TO MEDICAL STAFF
- Acts as liaison between physician and patient care team.

TO OWN NURSE MANAGER
- Shares appropriate communications with unit personnel.
- Ensures adequate staffing.

- Makes out patient care assignments.
- Helps with budget planning; operate unit within budget.

TO DEPARTMENT PERSONNEL

- Holds regular unit personnel meetings.
- Promotes an environment in which the patient-care team can work cooperatively toward objectives.
- Provides an opportunity for personnel staff development.
- Counsels personnel when necessary.

TO COMMITTEES

- Participates actively in selected committee activities.

TO OTHER ORGANIZATIONS

- Maintains membership in appropriate professional organizations.

TO SELF

- Participates in continuing education programs.

Significant Job Segments

- Patient care
- Medical staff
- Staffing
- Budget
- Meetings
- Subordinate development
- Self-development

Position Title: DATA PROCESSING MANAGER

Duties and Responsibilities

- Establishes departmental objectives.
- Schedules operations.
- Protects and maintains present equipment.
- Recommends new or modified equipment.
- Provides timely and pertinent reports.
- Administers tape library.
- Conducts departmental meetings.
- Administers company personnel policies.
- Hires, orients, and trains new personnel.
- Trains and develops employees.
- Handles employee suggestions and problems.
- Evaluates employee performance.

Significant Job Segments

- Objectives
- Operations
- Equipment
- Reports
- Tape library
- Meetings
- Personnel

Position Title: SALES MANAGER, CUSTOMER SERVICE PARTS

Duties and Responsibilities

- Supervises repair parts order analysts to ensure the expeditious writing and processing of parts orders.
- Provides instructions and guidance on difficult parts identification problems.
- Oversees warrantee parts activities to ensure proper crediting of return parts and fulfillment of vendor warranty obligations, and to alleviate problems regarding warrantee claims and related billings.
- Monitors correspondence procedures required to acknowledge parts and orders.
- Advises customers of order and price changes.
- Monitors the inventory and replenishment of parts at the company's bonded warehouses.
- Organizes and expedites the maintenance of up-to-date references, price lists, and files essential to service customers.
- Interviews, selects, trains, counsels, evaluates, and assigns work to clerical and technical personnel.
- Prepares reports.
- Helps develop objectives and budget.
- Operates within budget.

Significant Job Segments

- Orders
- Warrantees
- Customer contacts
- Personnel

- Reports
- Budget

Position Title: MANAGER, MANUFACTURING ENGINEERING

Duties and Responsibilities
- Documents all manufacturing engineering procedures, including routing cards, CRT update, engineering change notices, form design and modification, and any other required new procedures that are repeatable and necessary for future reference.
- Develops and implements procedures for an effective bonus incentive system.
- Directs the Idea Action Program in analyzing suggestions and computing awards.
- Oversees the packaging function that is responsible for the design and purchase specification of packaging material and the procedures for the actual packaging operation.
- Manages a waste and scrap program to include sales of scrap material, recycling scrap where possible, and solution of scrap and waste problems.
- Conducts special projects on plant operations and functions.
- Handles employee relations function for the department.

Significant Job Segments
- Documentation
- Bonus system
- Idea Action Program
- Packaging function
- Scrap program
- Employee relations

Determining Job Segments Without Job Descriptions

In organizations that do not have up-to-date job descriptions, the supervisor should sit down with the employee and discuss the job. The first step is to list all the duties and responsibilities that would apply to any person doing the job. If more than one person is doing the same job, the supervisor should conduct a meeting with all the employees to agree on duties and responsibilities. If the number of people is too large for a meeting, it is advisable to meet with a representative sample of the group.

When agreement has been reached on all the duties and responsibilities, the next step is to agree on the significant job segments. Again, the group approach should be used if more than one person is doing the same job.

In seeking agreement on the significant job segments, there are three different approaches that might be used:

1. The manager and employees independently list the significant job segments and then discuss them to reach understanding and agreement.
2. The manager makes a tentative list and presents it to the employees for reaction, modification, and agreement.
3. The employees make a tentative list and present it to the manager for reaction, modification, and agreement.

It doesn't make much difference which of the three approaches is used as long as understanding and agreement are reached. There is a possibility that the second choice will not be as effective as the other two because employees may be reluctant to challenge the "tentative" list made by the manager. Also, the involvement of the employee in choices 1 and 3 will probably create a climate in which the employee is more highly motivated toward the entire performance review process.

Summary

The first step in the performance review process is to clarify what's expected of the employee. The first part of this is for manager and employee to agree on the significant job segments that should be appraised. Typically, from six to eight segments should be identified. If job descriptions are available, they should be used as a basis for selecting the significant job segments. If not, a list of duties and responsibilities should be prepared. In order to be sure that the significant job segments are clear and agreed on, they should be jointly determined by manager and employee. The next step in the process of clarifying what's expected is to develop standards of performance for each significant job segment.

Standards of Performance

Standards of performance are an important and often neglected element in the performance review process. While significant job segments describe what needs to be done, standards of performance describe how well it must be done. The two of them together clarify what's expected of the employee. This clarification is necessary to guide the behavior of the employee as well as to provide a basis for appraisal.

Defining Standards of Performance

There is a difference of opinion among performance appraisal experts on the exact meaning of standards of performance. Some use the definition "the conditions that will exist when the job segment is well done." Others use the definition "the conditions that will exist when the job segment is done in an acceptable manner." Although the difference between "well done" and "acceptable" seems to be slight, the difference is very significant. The following two examples illustrate the difference.

Example 1

Here are some facts about the percentage of manufactured parts that were classified as scrap in a manufacturing plant. The figures refer to the past six months.

1. The best the percentage has been is 2 percent for a one-week period. This happened on two occasions.
2. It went as high as 15 percent for a one-week period. This is considered uncontrolled.
3. Except for these three one-week periods, it has varied from 3 percent to 10 percent on a weekly basis. The 3 percent figure occurred three times, and the 10 percent occurred twice.
4. The average weekly figure for the past six months has been 7 percent.
5. From 3 to 4 percent is considered excellent.

At what level should the standard be set? Mark your estimate before reading further.

2%   3%   4%   5%   6%   7%   8%   9%   10%

Example 2

Here are some facts about a daily report in an office. The figures are for the past six months.

1. Ideally, there should be no errors such as miscalculations and wrong entries, because this causes extra work and delay.
2. The best record for a week was one error. This occurred only once.
3. The report is sufficiently complex and frequent that as many as four errors are usually made per week, even by thoroughly experienced people. This you can live with.
4. When errors reach the level of six per week, the finance department complains because of the excessive amount of time needed to correct the errors.
5. The worst record for one week by an experienced employee was seven. This occurred only once. Six errors were made twice during the past six months.
6. There has been an average of 4.1 errors per week for the past six months.

At what level of errors per week do you think the standard should be set? Mark your estimate before reading further.

0   1   2   3   4   5   6

If standard of performance is defined as the conditions that will exist when the job is *well done,* the standards should probably be set at 4 percent scrap for Example 1 and two errors per week for Example 2. If standard of performance is defined as the conditions that will exist when the job is done in an acceptable manner, the standards should be set at 7 percent scrap for Example 1 and four errors per week for Example 2.

This book uses the definition "the conditions that will exist when the job segment is done in an *acceptable* manner." This means that the answers to the examples are 7 percent scrap and four errors per week.

The reason for this definition is that it provides a great deal of opportunity for the employee to exceed the standard and be recognized for it. It also means that performance is unsatisfactory if the standard is not met. If the other definition is used and the standard is met only when the job is well done, many satisfactory employees would not meet the standard, and this might have a negative effect on their attitude and desire to improve.

Characteristics of Standards

There are eight characteristics of effective standards:

1. *They are based on the job and not the person(s) in the job.* Standards of performance should be established for the job itself regardless of who occupies the job. For example, the job of marketing analyst or production foreman may be a job that a number of people perform. There should be one set of standards for the job, not one set for every person doing that particular job.

Standards of performance are different from objectives. Objectives should be set for an individual, rather than for a job. And a typical characteristic of an objective or goal is that it should be challenging. Therefore, a manager who has several employees who do the same job will have one set of standards for the job but may have different objectives for each person, based on that person's experience, skills, and past performance. For example, the objective for a mediocre performer may be the same as the standard, while the objective for an outstanding employee may be much higher than standard.

2. *They are achievable.* This characteristic is directly related to the definition described earlier. It means that practically all employees on the job should be able to reach the standard. (An exception is a new employee who is learning the job. The standard may not apply until the employee has passed the probationary period.) Most production standards are set so that practically everyone can meet the standard and many employees can reach 125 percent of standard.

In the 1980 Winter Olympics, at Lake Placid, New York, there were two ski hills. One was called the 70-Meter Hill and the other was called the 90-Meter Hill. The distance referred to the length of the jump by the skiers. Nearly all the competing skiers exceeded the 70 meters and the 90 meters, and many of them jumped from 20 to 30 meters beyond. The standard (70 meters or 90 meters) was much lower than the objective as well as the performance of the competitors.

3. *They are understood.* It almost goes without saying that the standard should be clear to manager and employee alike. Unfortunately, there is often confusion between the two parties on the exact meaning of a standard.

4. *They are agreed on.* Both manager and employee should agree that the standard is fair. This is very important in motivating an employee. It is also important because it becomes the basis for evaluation.

5. *They are as specific and as measurable as possible.* Some people feel that standards *must be* specific and measurable. They insist that they must be stated in numbers, percentages, dollars, or some other form that can be quantifiably measured. Every effort should be made to do this, but if it can't be done, the standard *should be* stated as specifically as possible even if subjective judgment must be used to evaluate performance against it. Early in a performance review program, it might seem impossible to state standards in measurable terms. With practice and experience, it may be possible to be specific on all or nearly all standards.

6. *They are time oriented.* It should be clear whether the standard is to be accomplished by a specific date or whether it is ongoing.

7. *They are written.* Both manager and employee should have a written copy of the standards that are agreed on. In this way, they won't have to rely on memory, and the standard can be a constant reminder to both parties.

8. *They are subject to change.* Because standards should be achievable and agreed on, they should be periodically evaluated and changed if necessary. The need to change may be new methods, new equipment, new materials, or changes in other significant job factors. But they should not be changed just because a performer is not meeting the standard.

Who Should Set Standards?

Because standards are to be clear and agreed on, there is good reason to involve employees in setting their own standards. Another reason for this involvement is to motivate the employee to put forth maximum effort to achieve and even exceed the standard. Helping to set the standards will probably result in a higher degree of commitment.

If only one person is doing a particular job, the manager and the employee should jointly set the standards. If more than one person is doing the same job, all the people on that job, or at least a representative group, should be involved. (In this respect, setting standards is just like determining significant job segments.) Where differences of opinion exist, the manager must have the final say. The manager should make every effort, however, to get the employees to agree that the standard is fair.

There are three ways of getting employee involvement in setting standards:

1. The manager considers all factors, prepares tentative standards, and discusses them with employees to get agreement. The manager must listen to them and be willing to change the standards if the employees' suggestions warrant a change.
2. The employees set their own tentative standards and bring them to the manager for agreement. Employees should be told in advance that their recommendations will not necessarily be accepted.
3. The manager and the employees independently set standards for significant job segments. These standards are compared and discussed to reach agreement.

The first approach is probably the least effective because employees might be reluctant to disagree with the tentative standards set by the manager. Often a manager who develops tentative standards becomes defensive and impatient with employees who challenge them. If this first approach is to be effective, the manager must be sure to create a climate in which employees feel free to disagree and in which the tentative standards are subject to change.

The second approach can be effective if the manager is knowledgeable enough to judge the standards suggested by the employee. It puts the major part of the responsibility on the employee, which is apt to create a commitment to achieve or exceed the standards.

The third approach is probably the best because each party has given some time and effort to the creation of fair standards. Their discussion should result in the best standards.

Sometimes an outside person such as a consultant or personnel director can effectively conduct a meeting between manager and subordinates to establish standards. This neutral party can keep the discussion objective so that good standards are developed and rapport is maintained between manager and employees.

How Many Standards?

This question is similar to "How many significant job segments?" There is no magic number, nor is there any rule of thumb that says it all depends on the job. The main factor that determines the number of standards is the manager. How many standards does he feel are needed to clarify what is expected of an employee? If two standards will do it (say, quantity and quality), then that should be sufficient. If it takes ten or twenty pages to define the standards, then that's how many there should be. There is an advantage to having many, rather than few. This not only gives an employee a clearer understanding of the total job but also allows the manager to appraise many different facets of the job and to pinpoint an employee's areas of strength, as well as those needing improvement. Therefore, an organization should not put a limit on the number of standards that should be developed for a job.

Following are samples of standards of performance that have been developed for segments of different jobs in a variety of organizations.

Position: PRODUCTION FOREMAN

Significant Job Segments	Standards of Performance
1. Safety	1. Monthly safety meetings are conducted in accordance with company schedules. 2. Safe operating procedures are followed by all employees. 3. Regular monthly inspections are held in the department in accordance with the approved checklist. 4. Action is taken within five days to correct any unsafe condition. 5. Monthly safety reports are submitted by the 5th of the following month.
2. Controlling costs	1. Waste and scrap are kept below 2 percent of total production. 2. One cost-saving improvement per month is initiated and put into operation. 3. Overtime costs are held to a maximum of 3 percent of direct labor costs. 4. All purchases are made in the most economical manner according to a buying plan. 5. Overhead costs are kept within budget limitations. 6. Salary controls are exercised in accordance with the salary administration plan. 7. The ratio of productivity to costs is improved by 1 percent every six months.

3. Developing employees	1. New employees are inducted and trained in accordance with a definite plan.
	2. Performance reviews are held with all employees on an annual basis.
	3. The appraisal and performance improvement plan aspects of the performance review program are reviewed with the manager.
	4. Discussions are held with employees at least quarterly to see that performance improvement takes place according to plan.
	5. Responsibilities and authority are delegated to employees on a planned basis.

Position: EMPLOYMENT SUPERVISOR

Significant Job Segments	Standards of Performance
1. Recruiting	1. Ninety percent of requisitions for qualified employees are filled within three weeks of date of requisition.
	2. Each employee is recruited at a cost lower than the cost of hiring one employee through a commercial placement agency.
	3. Current file of qualified applicants is maintained to fill recurring job openings.
	4. Job inquiries are answered within two working days of receipt.

Position: OFFICE SUPERVISOR

Significant Job Segments	Standards of Performance
1. Written communication	1. All correspondence is answered within one week of its receipt.
	2. All written communication is handled so that there is minimal misunderstanding.
	3. All interdepartmental and intradepartmental memorandums are answered within two working days of receipt.

4. All official memorandums are posted and/or e-mailed, approved, and returned to the department head within one week of receiving them.
5. Minutes of officially called meetings are sent to participants within five days after the meeting.

Position: REGIONAL SALES MANAGER

Significant Job Segments	*Standards of Performance*
1. Developing employees	
A. Conducts performance reviews	1. Performance reviews are conducted with all employees according to the procedure approved by the sales manager.
	2. For new employees, job duties and standards are clarified within the first three months of employment.
	3. A complete performance review is conducted within nine months of hire of each new employee.
B. Coaches	1. Employees are coached and worked with on a day-to-day basis to help them perform better on their present jobs.
	2. Follow-up is conducted to ensure implementation of performance improvement plan.
	3. Selected assignments are delegated to employees to help develop them for greater responsibilities.
C. Trains in products	1. Employees understand the products, procedures, programs, and policies that are pertinent to their work.
	2. District sales managers know how to use these items.
	3. District sales managers put pertinent items into operation.

D. Counsels   1. Employees feel that regional sales managers
                           are readily available and glad to discuss
                           problems with them.
                        2. All personal conversations are kept
                           confidential.

E. General   1. Employees clearly understand their jobs.
                        2. Employees are qualified and skilled to
                           perform their jobs.
                        3. Employees know how well they are doing
                           and what improvement needs to be made.
                        4. Employees are consistently improving
                           performance on their present jobs.

Position: CORPORATE UNIVERSITY MANAGER

Significant Job Segments	*Standards of Performance*

1. Training Classes	1. Training needs are determined by using one or more of the following:
	  a. Surveys of potential participants
	  b. Advisory committee meetings
	  c. Discussion and/or correspondence with key people
	2. Program objectives are established on the basis of needs.
	3. Program content is developed on the basis of objectives.
	4. Speakers are selected and coached.
	  a. Teachers have knowledge and teaching skills.
	  b. Teachers are oriented on program objectives and participants.
	5. Coordination.
	  a. A minimum of forty-five program days are held per year.
	  b. Facilities, introduction of leaders, visual aids, and materials are effectively coordinated.

6. Evaluation.
   a. Standard reaction sheet is used for each program.
   b. Standard of 3.7 on a 4.0 scale is achieved in 90 percent of the programs.

2. Performance Review	1. All salaried personnel are reviewed annually.
	2. All reviewers receive fourteen hours of training on performance reviews by January 1.
	3. All completed performance improvement plans are received by February 15.
	4. Confidential files are maintained on all performance reviews and made available only to authorized persons.

Position: DEPARTMENT HEAD

Significant Job Segments	*Standards of Performance*
1. Planning	1. Suggested items for next year's expense budget are submitted by September 15.
	2. Suggested capital expenditures for next year are submitted by September 15.
	3. Specific annual objectives are established for next year by December 1.
	4. A report on specific accomplishments for the past year is submitted by January 20.
	5. Long-range plans covering a five-year period are prepared by December 15 and updated yearly.
	6. Daily assignments are given to accomplish a minimum of 85 percent of established schedules.

Position: DIVISION MANAGER

Significant Job Segments	*Standards of Performance*
1. Communication	1. Managerial and functional staff are kept informed of all important or unusual conditions or trends that have a bearing on the company's interests so that no such matters come first to their attention from outside sources.
	2. All regularly scheduled managers' conferences are attended by division manager unless ill or away. Pertinent information based on field experience is relayed to other managers and staff members in attendance, and appropriate opinions are expressed to contribute to the discussion of subjects under consideration.
	3. Meetings are held with division staff and district supervisory personnel within ten days following each managers' conference to relay items of information from the conference and to discuss pertinent topics of local interest.
	4. Similar meetings are held within one week in each of the districts in the division.
	5. New developments and pertinent information such as company plans and policy changes are relayed to all division personnel involved within one week of the manager's receiving such information.
	6. Employees feel that division manager is personally available to them to discuss problems or ideas.

Summary

Standards of performance are defined as conditions that will exist when the job has been done in an acceptable manner. They have two purposes. First, they guide the behavior of an employee to accomplish the standards that have been established. According to James L. Hayes, former president of the American Management Association and an internationally known expert on standards of performance,

> If you go through the exercise of establishing standards of performance with your employees and clarify what your expectations are, it is a worthwhile exercise even if you never appraise their performance. This is because most people want to do an acceptable job.

The second reason for standards of performance is to provide a basis against which the performance of an employee can be effectively and fairly appraised. Unless clear standards of performance are established, appraisals are too often biased by feelings and subjective evaluation. Regardless of the approach and forms that are used in a program on performance appraisal and review, the process of clarifying what's expected is essential if the program is going to be effective. Standards of performance are the best way to do this.

Effective standards of performance are based on the job and are achievable, understood, agreed on, specific and measurable, time oriented, written, and subject to change.

So that the standards can be properly set and employees are motivated to meet or exceed them, employees should be involved in setting their own standards. In case of disagreement, the manager must make the final decision.

There is no minimum or maximum number of standards that should be set for a job. Having many standards helps the employee understand more clearly what is expected and also helps the manager pinpoint specific strengths and areas needing improvement. The manager and the employee should decide the number of standards that is both appropriate and practical.

CHAPTER 3

The Appraisal and the Interview

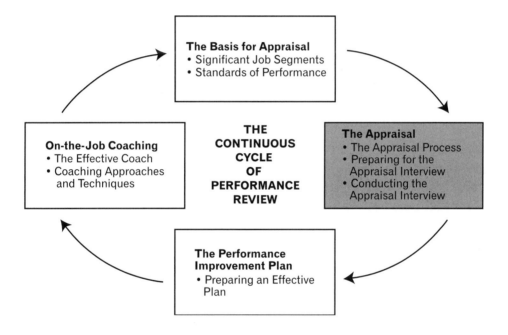

The Appraisal Process

If an effective job is done in clarifying what's expected in terms of significant job segments and standards of performance, the appraisal by the manager becomes quite easy and objective. It is a matter of comparing actual performance with definite standards. And the more specific and measurable the standards, the more objective the appraisal.

Two Traps to Avoid

In the book *Management by Objectives,* George Odiorne warns that two kinds of flaws may exist in a performance appraisal if the standards are vague: the halo effect and the horns effect.[1]

The Halo Effect. The halo effect is the tendency of the manager to over-rate a favored employee. This can happen for a variety of reasons:

1. *Effect of Past Record.* Because the person has done good work in the distant past, performance is assumed to be O.K. in the recent past, too. Good opinions tend to carry over into the current rating period.

2. *Compatibility.* There's a tendency to rate people whom we find pleasing of manner and personality more highly than they deserve. Those who agree with us, who nod their heads when we talk, or who—even better—make notes of our words: these people get better ratings than their performance justifies.

3. *Effect of Recency.* An outstanding job done last week or yesterday can offset a mediocre performance over the rest of the year.

4. *The One-Asset Person.* The glib talker, the person with an impressive appearance or an advanced degree, or the graduate of the manager's own alma mater gets a more favorable rating than the person who lacks these often irrelevant attributes.

5. *The Blind-Spot Effect.* This is the case where the supervisor doesn't see certain types of defects because they are just like his or her own. For example, the supervisor who loves accounting may overrate another detail person.

6. *The High-Potential Effect.* We sometimes judge the person's paper record, rather than what she has accomplished for the organization.

7. *The No-Complaints Bias.* Here the appraiser treats no news as good news. The employee who has no complaints and says that everything is terrific is likely to go over well.

The Horns Effect. This is the reverse of the halo effect—the tendency to rate a person lower than the circumstances justify. Some specific causes of this are these:

1. *The manager is a perfectionist.* Because the expectations of the manager are so high, she is often disappointed and rates an employee lower than deserved.

2. *The employee is contrary.* Here the manager vents private irritation with the employee's tendency to disagree too often on too many issues.

3. *The oddball effect.* All the lip service to nonconformity seldom counts when appraisal time comes around. The oddball, the maverick, the nonconformist get low ratings simply because they are different.

4. *Membership in a weak team.* A good player on a weak team ends up with lower ratings than he would have gotten if he were on a winning team.

5. *The guilt-by-association effect.* The person who isn't really known well by the manager is often judged by the company he keeps.

6. *The dramatic-incident effect.* A recent goof can wipe out the effect of months of good work and give a person a lower rating than deserved.

7. *The personality-trait effect.* The employee who is too cocky, too brash, too meek, or too passive or who lacks some trait the manager associates with good employees suffers in the appraisal.

8. *The self-comparison effect.* The person who does the job differently from the way the manager did it when she still had that job suffers more than a person whose job the manager has never done.

If standards of performance have been effectively established, both the halo and horns effects can be eliminated or at least drastically reduced.

Gathering Information

From one appraisal time to the next, a manager should be gathering information that will make the appraisal fair and accurate. If this is not done, the appraisal may be based on hazy memory or on only the most recent behavior and accomplishments of the employee.

J. C. Flanagan developed an objective approach for gathering data for the appraisal. He called it the critical incident method.[2] This technique relies on the collection of specific observable job incidents that are judged to be critical because they are related directly to either good or poor job performance. After the incidents are collected and tabulated, components are grouped under one of the headings in a specially designed performance record.

The performance record is accompanied by a manual that describes and illustrates each of the sixteen critical requirements. The supervisor records each incident on either the "effective" (blue) or the "ineffective" (red) half of the page for the employee involved. The manual states that to be critical, an incident must be directly observed by the supervisor and must clearly show either outstanding or less-than-satisfactory performance.

In his experience with the Delco-Remy Division of General Motors, Flanagan found that most of the recorded incidents were positive. There was speculation that the manager would be much more apt to record the negative incidents, but this was not true.

The critical incident method involves three basic steps: (1) completing the performance record as critical incidents occur; (2) summarizing them for the rating period; and (3) conducting a performance review interview with the employee. Flanagan recommends that this three-phase program be carried out at six-month intervals, and he suggests further that the performance review interview take from half an hour to an hour. Summarizing his method, he says:

> A performance record is not a yardstick. It is not a rating method. It is a procedure for collecting significant facts about employee performance. These facts are gathered in such a way that they will be of maximum use to supervisors and management, both in improving the employee's understanding of the requirements of his present job and in developing his potential for more responsible positions. It is not simply a new form but a new approach.

If the critical incident method is used, managers should be sure to look for both positive and negative incidents. Otherwise, the appraisal will become biased and the employee will be unfairly appraised.

In gathering information, the manager should have one objective: to make an accurate appraisal of performance. He can get this information from two major sources:

1. *Performance Records.* These include records on quantity of production, quality of work, compliance with deadlines and schedules, safety, actual costs versus budget costs, absenteeism, and the number of complaints from customers or coworkers.

2. *Other People Who Have Had Dealings with the Employee.* This could include the supervisor, staff personnel, people served by the employee, and even people in other departments with whom the employee worked. If the organization uses project teams on which the employee has served, the project leader should be contacted. This should be as objective as possible. Instead of asking, "How do you feel about Harry?" it's better to ask, "What kind of service has Harry given you?"

or "How would you evaluate Harry's performance in regard to this issue?"

In other words, the more sources used, the better. But each source should be carefully selected to provide objective data. All these data should then be analyzed and compared with the standards of performance to arrive at the most accurate appraisal.

Appraisal Categories and Scales

The appraisal process requires some type of scale to allow the manager to differentiate between different levels of performance. Perhaps the simplest and best approach is to use the following four categories to appraise performance on each standard:

DNMS   Does not meet standard
MS   Meets standard
ES   Exceeds standard
O   Outstanding

The appraisal form looks like this:

Significant Job Segments	Standards of Performance	DNMS	MS	ES	O	Comments

Some organizations use such words as *unsatisfactory, satisfactory, outstanding,* and *superior.* Other organizations prefer such terms as *unacceptable, acceptable, good, very good,* and *excellent.*

Some military units use such words as *good, excellent, outstanding,* and *superior.* Here there are two words that mean something better than *excellent,* so *excellent* becomes a term that means about the same as *marginal* or *acceptable.*

Some organizations prefer a five- or ten-point scale, with 1 at the low end of the scale meaning *poor* or *unsatisfactory* and 5 or 10 at the top level of the scale to mean *outstanding* or *superior.*

Still other organizations try to describe the gradations by saying such things as:

Poor: Consistently unsatisfactory. Doesn't come close to meeting standard.

Fair: Occasionally meets standard. Usually is slightly below standard.

Good: Consistently meets standard. Rarely exceeds standard.

Very Good: Consistently above standard. Occasionally doesn't meet standard. Occasionally far above standard.

Excellent: Consistently far above standard.

Other categories and scales are used in the examples in this book.

If the purpose of performance appraisal is to improve performance, the word *average* should not be used. This word invites comparison with other people, rather than with the standard. In order to improve performance, it is important to identify, for each person, the level of performance for each standard. This will reveal strengths as well as areas that need improvement. If the purpose of the appraisal is to determine salary increases, rather than to improve performance, then the word *average* may be used. In this context, individuals' performances are compared with each other.

Self-Appraisal

The concept of self-appraisal is required in some programs, left optional in some, and discouraged or prohibited in others. In a situation where the employee does not complete a self-appraisal, the supervisor makes out the appraisal form, calls in the employee for the appraisal interview, and tries to get both understanding and acceptance of the appraisal from the employee. The employee usually comes to the interview without any specific preparation and is perhaps fearful that it will be an unpleasant experience. He may have made an informal self-appraisal, but not one in writing. The employee is apt to be on the defensive because the manager reads off the appraisal and asks him to agree or to substantiate any disagreement. Many employees do not speak freely because they lack information to substantiate their judgments of themselves or because they are afraid to disagree with the manager. Therefore, they may very well express agreement—or rather, refrain from expressing disagreement—even though they don't really agree. And the manager naively feels that both understanding and agreement have been reached.

If the employee completes a self-appraisal, preferably on the same form the manager uses, the two of them can sit side by side and compare their appraisals. This can create a relaxed climate in which the objective is to arrive at an accurate appraisal. If both of them have honestly tried to be as objective as possible, and if the significant job segments and standards of performance have been clearly stated, the appraisals shouldn't be far apart.

The concept of self-appraisal says to the employee: "Your input is important. Maybe you know some things about your performance I don't know. I want to be sure that you have a chance to communicate them to me. And I'll listen to you and consider your input before arriving at a final appraisal."

Several factors should be kept in mind if self-appraisals are going to be used:

1. Employees should be given enough advance notice so that a fair self-appraisal can be made. A minimum of three weeks should be allowed.
2. Employees should be told the reasons for the self-appraisal and how it will be used in the interview.
3. Specific instructions should be given employees about the form to use and what to do.
4. Employees should be urged to make an objective appraisal and not to be overly aggressive (rating themselves higher than justified) or shy (rating themselves lower than justified).
5. Managers should assure employees that the self-appraisal will be used to help arrive at a fair appraisal.

Summary

The appraisal process must be done in a systematic and objective manner, by first gathering data from various sources and then comparing performance with standards that have been previously set. It is important for the employee to accept the appraisal as fair. The best way to accomplish this is to have the employee prepare a self-appraisal that can then be compared with the appraisal by the manager. Free and open discussion also helps to arrive at a fair appraisal agreed on and accepted by both parties. In case of disagreement, the manager must make the final appraisal, but in most cases agreement can be reached without the manager's exercising this authority.

Preparing for the Appraisal Interview

If the interview is going to be effective, the appraiser must prepare. The first step is to determine the objectives to accomplish, and the second is to make preparations to accomplish them.

Objectives to Accomplish

In the appraisal interview, there are five major objectives:

1. To reach agreement on the performance of the employee
2. To identify strengths
3. To identify performance areas that need to be improved
4. To agree on a performance improvement plan for one or more areas that need improvement
5. To agree on what's expected (that is, significant job segments and standards of performance) for the next appraisal period

Because there are so many objectives, it is very difficult to accomplish all of them in one interview. As suggested earlier, it is usually better to plan for two or three interviews. For example, the first interview might cover objectives 1, 2, and 3. The second interview might include objective 4, and a third interview objective 5. It probably wouldn't take any more time than if it were done in one interview. And both parties could adequately prepare for each interview.

Preparation by the Manager

Before the interview takes place, the manager should make the following preparations:

1. *Decide on the best time.* The best time is when both parties are able to spend time together without interruption, so it is a good idea for the manager to suggest a time and get approval from the employee.

2. *Decide on the best place.* A private office is the best place. It may be the office of the manager or a neutral place. It should be a private place where the door can be closed and people can't look in and see

what's going on. Also, it should be a comfortable place where both parties can relax.

3. *Prepare the facilities.* Arrange the furniture so that the employee will feel at ease. Perhaps the chairs should be side by side instead of across the desk from each other. If possible, have coffee or water available.

4. *Gather information and materials.* Make a complete and objective appraisal as described earlier in this chapter. Have the forms and information on hand so that they are readily available during the interview.

5. *Plan the opening.* Decide whether to talk about a current event—such as sports, politics, or weather—or to begin by stating the purpose of the interview. Use whatever approach is most natural and will create the best climate for the interview.

6. *Plan the approach.* Here are some alternatives to consider:
   (a) Begin with strengths and then discuss job segments needing improvement.
   (b) Go straight through the form, give your appraisal, and discuss one item at a time to get agreement before going ahead to the next item.
   (c) Ask the employee for his or her appraisal before giving your own. You could do this for the entire form or on each item.
   (d) Alternate between yourself and the employee as to who gives the appraisal first.

There is no right or wrong approach. Your approach might depend on whether the employee has made a self-appraisal. Remember that the objective is to get agreement, so use whatever approach is best for you.

7. *Give the employee appropriate advance notice.* The employee should have enough time to prepare for the interview and should clearly understand the time, place, objectives, and probable length of the interview.

8. *Plan the conclusion.* Know how and when you want to end the interview. For example, you may want to agree on the total appraisal, three strengths, three areas needing improvement, and one performance area to improve. Then you may want to summarize and describe what will happen next. For example, you may want to close the interview by saying, "Brad, before we get together again, I'd like you to think about this one area of improvement that you and I think is most important. Jot down some things that you can do. Also, jot down some

things that I can do to help you. I'll do the same. Let's get together to develop a specific performance improvement plan that we both think will work. How about two weeks from today at the same time and place? Does that sound O.K. to you?"

In some instances, all the objectives may be accomplished in one interview. In other cases, the first interview may end with an agreement on the final appraisal. The second interview would accomplish the objectives of agreeing on three strengths, three areas requiring improvement, and the one area to be covered in the performance improvement plan. A third interview would develop the performance improvement plan and agree on significant job segments and standards of performance for the next period of time.

Any of these approaches can be effective. The important factor is that the manager should decide in advance what should be accomplished in the interview and should prepare to conclude accordingly.

9. *Guarantee that there are no interruptions.* Be sure that there are no interruptions by phone calls or visitors.

10. *Avoid inappropriate preparation.* When I worked for a large mineral and chemical corporation in the early 1960s, my first job was to develop a corporate performance review program. The program was first introduced and implemented at the Carlsbad, New Mexico, plant. After that, we implemented it in a plant at Bartow, Florida, and one in San José, California, as well as in the sales department at Skokie, Illinois. It was based on some of the principles and approaches described in this book. Emphasis was on the manager and employee working together to improve job performance.

A near-disaster occurred when a firm of consulting psychologists tried to sell its services to management. The psychologists wanted to coach every manager before the manager conducted the appraisal interview with a employee. Their philosophy was to describe to the manager the personality and other characteristics of the employee. Then, according to the psychologists, the manager would be able to conduct an effective interview on the basis of this knowledge.

The approach would have been detrimental for two reasons. First, it would have bogged down the entire program because every manager would have had to be counseled before every interview. Second, the managers would not have been able to conduct straightforward performance appraisal interviews. Rather, they would have been required (or at least encouraged) to conduct interviews the way they had been told by the psychologists. This would probably have been contrary to the practical approach we built into the program, where manager and employee sat down side by side and discussed openly and frankly the past and future performance of the employee.

Fortunately, top management decided not to hire the psychologists, and the program was implemented as planned, with frank and open job-oriented interviews.

Another type of inappropriate preparation is for the manager to prepare to describe her own appraisal and to convince the employee that it is right. This creates a negative interview climate in which the employee is inhibited from being honest and open. Also, if the critical incident method is used for appraisal as described earlier, the manager should avoid using lots of examples of negative behavior to prove a point. This seriously hampers the interview's effectiveness by placing too much emphasis on past performance, rather than looking toward the future.

Preparation by the Employee

The employee must be given enough advance notice, as stated in item 7. In preparing for the interview, the employee should do the following:

1. Gather information related to past performance. This includes specific data on activities and accomplishments, as well as reasons why certain things weren't done or were done incorrectly.
2. Complete a self-appraisal if requested by the manager.
3. Arrange for work coverage while she is absent from the department. This is important so that the employee can concentrate on the interview and not worry about whether the job is being done properly.

Preparation Time

The amount of time required for preparation depends on various factors, including the forms that must be completed and discussed, the relationship and rapport that exist between manager and employee, previous performance review interviews between them, and whether manager and employee have jointly developed significant job segments and standards of performance.

Summary

Preparation for the appraisal interview should be made by both manager and employee. The manager should determine the objectives to accomplish, arrange for proper facilities, notify the employee, and plan the specific approach to use. The employee should be prepared to participate in the discussion in order to arrive at a fair appraisal. If a specific self-appraisal is required, the employee should be given plenty of time to prepare.

Conducting the Appraisal Interview

The purpose of the appraisal interview is to discuss performance, not personality. It is future oriented, rather than past oriented. Emphasis should be on what the employee will do in the future and not on what has been done in the past. However, a discussion of past performance is essential as the basis for the future.

Ten Guidelines to Remember

The following general principles apply to all performance interviews regardless of the form that is used or whether a self-appraisal has been completed.

    1. *Establish and maintain rapport.* Rapport can be defined as the climate in which the interview takes place. First of all, as mentioned earlier, the location of the interview is important. It should be a place where both people can feel relaxed. The chairs should be comfortable. There should be a minimum of noise. No one else should be able to see the two people. If it will help to put the employee at ease, the manager and the employee should sit alongside each other rather than face each other across the desk. The words as well as the nonverbal communications of the manager should make it clear that two-way communication will take place and that the employee should speak freely and frankly. A cup of coffee might help to create this comfortable climate.

    It is debatable whether to begin the interview by talking about hobbies or some current event or whether to begin by saying, "As you know, the purpose of this interview is to . . . ." If the two people have a common hobby, that may be a good place to start. Or if there was an unusual political or sporting event that just happened, that may be a good opener.

    Socializing for a few minutes is well worth the time if it creates rapport. The following list contrasts an interview climate characterized by rapport to an interview climate that lacks it:

Rapport	Lack of Rapport
At ease, relaxed	Nervous, fearful, anxious
Comfortable	Uncomfortable
Friendly, warm	Formal, cold
Not afraid to speak freely and frankly	Afraid to speak openly
Believing, trusting	Challenging
Listening	Interrupting
Understanding	Misunderstanding
Open-minded	Closed-minded
Accepting criticism without resentment	Resenting criticism
Disagreeing without offending	Arguing, downgrading

2. *Clearly explain the purpose of the interview.* Make it clear to the employee what you want to accomplish. State it in positive terms, such as: "The purpose of the interview today is for us to discuss your performance and agree on your strengths and areas that can be improved. Then we are going to talk about your future and how we can work together."

3. *Encourage the employee to talk.* The interview must include two-way communication. Some employees are eager to talk, while others are reluctant because of shyness or fear. The establishment of rapport helps to overcome this reluctance. In some situations, the manager must ask specific questions to get the employee to talk. In others, the employee talks freely with little encouragement.

4. *Listen and don't interrupt.* The word "listen" here means to *really listen.* It means more than merely keeping quiet or not talking. It is an active process of finding out the thoughts as well as the feelings of the other person. And if both parties start to talk at the same time, the manager should quit talking and encourage the employee to go ahead. This backing down is quite difficult for some managers, but it pays off in maintaining two-way communication throughout the interview. It tells the employee, "What you have to say is more important to me than what I have to say to you!"

5. *Avoid confrontation and argument.* Even though differences of opinions are expressed, the manager should avoid confrontation and argument. It is obvious to both parties that the manager has more authority and power than the employee. Therefore, there is a chance of

ending up in a win-lose situation where the manager wins and the employee loses. Unfortunately, winning by the manager can be very costly, because it can destroy rapport and result in the employee's deciding not to communicate freely and frankly. If this happens, the interview will not achieve its objectives and might even do more harm than good. By keeping the discussion free and open, a win-win situation can be created so that the needs of both people are met.

6. *Focus on performance, not personality.* This is a performance appraisal interview, and emphasis should be on performance, not personality. This does not mean that such items as attitude, integrity, dependability, appearance, or initiative are not mentioned. It means that these characteristics are mentioned only as they relate to performance.

7. *Focus on the future, not the past.* This does not mean that past performance is not discussed. But the emphasis is on what can be learned from the past that will help in the future.

8. *Emphasize strengths as well as areas to improve.* Every employee has strengths as well as areas of performance that can be improved. Don't ignore the strengths. Recognize and build on these strengths, and also discuss job segments that must be corrected if performance is to improve.

9. *Terminate the interview when advisable.* Don't hesitate to terminate an interview at any point if you think it's a good idea. Any number of reasons could justify the termination, including loss of rapport, the need for manager or employee to go somewhere, the end of the work day, lack of progress, fatigue, or an important interruption. If you end the interview before accomplishing all of the objectives you set, agree on when the interview will continue.

10. *Conclude on a positive note.* Be sure that the employee leaves the interview in a positive frame of mind instead of feeling resentful of the negative aspects of the discussion. After the interview is over, the employee should say (or at least feel), "Thanks. I'm glad we had a chance to get together and discuss any performance. Now I know where I stand and what I should do in the future. And I know that you are going to work with me."

A warm handshake at the conclusion of the interview is one way to end on a positive tone. Another is for the manager to say, "Thanks for coming in. I feel that this has been a very profitable discussion, and I know I can count on you in the future. I'll be glad to help you in any way I can."

Techniques for Successful Interviews

As explained earlier, there really shouldn't be any great surprises if the significant job segments and standards of performance have been clarified and agreed on as the basis for the appraisal. The employee's appraisal, whether mental or written, should be very close to the written appraisal by the manager.

The problem the manager faces is making sure he gets honest agreement or disagreement from the employee on the appraisal. Obviously, the establishment of rapport is essential for this. Specific interviewing techniques are also important. Here are some specific suggestions:

1. *Be open.* Show the form to the employee. Don't hide it.

2. *Explain your appraisal.* Describe how you arrived at it. If you checked records or talked to other people, say so. If you did it by yourself, say so. Also, be sure to emphasize that you want frank comments from the employee because your appraisal may not be accurate. Admit, for example, that the employee may have done some things you've forgotten or don't even know about.

3. *Be sure your appraisal is tentative.* Be willing to change your appraisal if the employee's input convinces you that you were wrong. Don't be afraid to admit a mistake.

4. *Summarize.* When the entire appraisal has been discussed, go over it with the employee. Have a copy made for the employee so that he or she has the same information you have.

All four of these techniques demonstrate to the employee that there is nothing secret about what you are doing. A manager simply wants to come up with a fair and accurate appraisal that will make it possible to work with the employee and help her improve performance in the future. The manager may want to start with strengths or with the first item on the appraisal form and go straight down the form. Whatever way is most natural and comfortable is the best way. After the discussion is ended, the entire appraisal should be summarized.

Using the Self-Appraisal

If the employee has made a written self-appraisal, it is easier for a manager to conduct an effective performance appraisal interview. The best way to start is to put both forms side by side and compare them. The manager can say, "You've made out an appraisal just as I have. Let's see where we agree and where we disagree. I'll read off my appraisal and you mark it on your form. Then you read off your appraisal and I'll mark it on my form."

After this has been done, it's helpful to start with the items where there is agreement, then go to items of disagreement. Ask the employee to explain his rationale. Then the manager can do the same. Through discussion, differences can be resolved and agreement reached on a fair appraisal.

Evaluating the Interview

After the interview has been completed, the manager should evaluate it to determine its effectiveness as well as to glean ideas for improving future interviews. Interviewers can evaluate a completed interview by asking themselves the following questions:

- If I had it to do over again, what changes would I make in my approach? What things would I cover that were omitted this time? What things would I omit that were discussed, perhaps unnecessarily?
- Who did most of the talking? Did I really listen to what the employee had to say?
- Was I satisfied with the interview? Do the employee and I understand each other better as a result?
- Do I feel that I'll be able to conduct my next interview more effectively?

Summary

Conducting the interview is one of the most important and difficult parts of a performance review program. Good preparation, as described in this section, is essential. In addition, there are specific interviewing approaches and techniques that can be used for maximum effectiveness. Here are ten important principles to remember:

1. Establish and maintain rapport.
2. Clearly explain the purpose of the interview.
3. Encourage the employee to talk.
4. Listen and don't interrupt.

5. Avoid confrontation and argument.
6. Focus on performance, not personality.
7. Focus on the future, not the past.
8. Emphasize strengths as well as areas to improve.
9. Terminate the interview when advisable.
10. Conclude on a positive note.

In addition to these principles, this section gave other interviewing suggestions. For example, openness is important. Show the appraisal form to the employee, and describe where you got the information and how you arrived at the ratings. Be willing to change the appraisal if the employee provides information to justify a change. Finally, summarize the appraisal discussion when it is over, and give a copy of the final completed form to the employee.

Notes

1. George Odiorne, *Management by Objectives* (New York: Pitman, 1965).
2. J. C. Flanagan and R. K. Burns, "The Employee Performance Record: A New Appraisal and Development Tool." *Harvard Business Review,* September–October 1955. Reprinted with permission.

CHAPTER 4

The Performance Improvement Plan

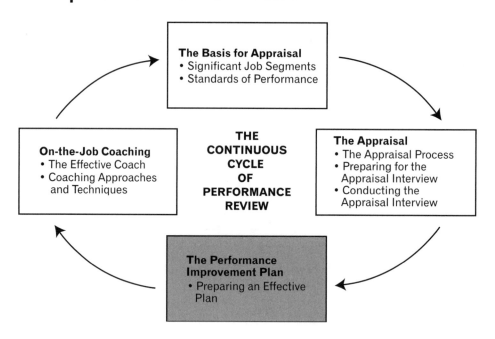

The Basis for Appraisal
• Significant Job Segments
• Standards of Performance

On-the-Job Coaching
• The Effective Coach
• Coaching Approaches
  and Techniques

THE CONTINUOUS CYCLE OF PERFORMANCE REVIEW

The Appraisal
• The Appraisal Process
• Preparing for the
  Appraisal Interview
• Conducting the
  Appraisal Interview

The Performance Improvement Plan
• Preparing an Effective
  Plan

Preparing an Effective Plan

A performance improvement plan is a specific course of action to be taken to improve the performance of the employee. It should describe what will be done, by whom, and when.

In the appraisal interview, segments of the job to be improved by the employee should be identified. The next step is to select the *one* segment of performance that should be worked on first. If too many are worked on, there is a good probability that the task will be over-whelming and nothing will be accomplished. The one job performance segment should be jointly determined by manager and employee. Four criteria should be used to select it:

1. What does the manager feel is most important? Perhaps the employee could improve a weakness that is causing serious problems, or maybe the manager wants improvement in an already strong area.
2. What area does the employee think should be worked on? This factor probably reveals the motivation of the employee to improve, because the employee usually won't pick an area that she does not want to improve.
3. What area of improvement would bring prompt results? This would provide a successful experience and could lead to improvement in other areas.
4. What area of improvement would have the greatest payoff in advantages versus time, energy, and money expended? This would be an objective decision based only on facts and logic.

The very process of jointly picking the one job segment to improve can build rapport and understanding between manager and employee.

Ingredients of a Plan

The performance improvement plan should meet four criteria:

1. *It should be practical.* The specifics of the plan should be related to the job performance to be improved. Reading a theoretical book or taking a three-credit university course on industrial psychology might not be practical.

2. *It should be time oriented.* Specific deadline dates should be set. These should be realistic and jointly determined.

3. *It should be specific.* It should clearly describe what will be done. For example, if the area to be improved is the quality of communication with employees, the reading of a book by the employee would be one action to take. The name of a specific book should be listed, instead of the statement "Read a book on communications."

4. *It should involve commitment.* Both manager and employee should be sold on the plan and committed to its implementation. They should agree that it will be done.

Requirements for Behavior Change

The performance improvement plan is designed to bring about a change in the behavior of the employee. If this change is going to take place, five requirements must be met:

1. *Desire.* The employee must want to change.

2. *Knowledge and Skill.* The employee must know what to do and also how to do it.

3. *Climate.* The employee must operate in a climate that provides an opportunity to behave in a different way. The most important factor in this climate is the manager. Managers can provide the following types of climate:

    (a) *Preventing.* This means that the manager does not allow the employee to do what he or she wants to do.

    (b) *Discouraging.* The manager doesn't say, "You can't," but does say, "I wouldn't recommend it," or "I wouldn't do it if I were you," or "I'm not saying you can't do it, but if you do it and it doesn't work out, you are in trouble!" These statements discourage a employee from changing behavior.

    (c) *Neutral.* The manager leaves it up to the employee. The typical attitude of the manager is: "I just want results. If you want to do it, it's up to you."

    (d) *Encouraging.* The manager says, "It sound like a good idea. Why don't you try it?"

    (e) *Requiring.* The manager says, "Do it and I'll help you."

It's pretty obvious that the climate must be neutral or better if the subordinate is going to change his behavior. If the manager establishes a preventing or discouraging climate, it is almost certain that no change in behavior will take place. Therefore, the entire process leading up to the desired change in behavior must build the right climate between manager and employee.

4. *Help and Support.* If an employee is going to improve, he will need encouragement and help. The person may be afraid to try something new because of fear of failure Or an employee may intend to try it but not get around to it unless encouraged. Also, the person may not have the confidence or skill to try it without encouragement and assistance. The help can come from the manager, from a training or personnel professional, or from both.

5. *Rewards.* People who know they will be rewarded for changing are apt to change. Also, if the rewards really come, they will be moti-

vated to change in the future. Rewards for changing behavior may be of a monetary or nonmonetary nature. Monetary rewards include salary increases, bonuses, or other financial incentives. Nonmonetary rewards include self-satisfaction, praise, increased responsibility, and more freedom and authority to act.

Who Develops the Plan?

Plans should be practical, time oriented, and specific. The implementation of the plan requires the commitment of both manager and employee. These requirements suggest and almost necessitate that the plan be jointly developed by manager and employee. In addition, a training and development professional may be required to help. Line managers and employees are able to work out special job assignments, but they usually do not know what books to read or conferences to attend. Training professionals can recommend these from experience.

How Should the Plan Be Developed?

When the need for improvement has been determined, the first step is to determine the causes of the problem. Why isn't performance as good as it could and should be? The problem may be with the manager, the employee, or the situation.

The employee may be doing something wrong or not doing what he should do. He may not understand what's expected; he may lack skill or motivation.

The manager could be doing counterproductive things that prevent the employee from performing to the maximum. Or the manager might not be doing something that would help the employee perform better. Some typical supervisor's mistakes are:

Doing What Shouldn't Be Done

Supervising too closely

Criticizing every mistake

Requiring the employee to come to the manager for all decisions and solutions to all problems

Putting undue pressure on the employee

Not Doing What Should Be Done

Not clarifying what's expected on the job

Not seeing that the employee has necessary skills to do the job

Not giving praise for a job well done

Not being available to the employee

Not listening and considering ideas of the employee

Not keeping the employee informed

Not taking a personal interest in the employee

Not encouraging the employee to grow through delegation, special assignments, and education

Not encouraging the employee to try out new ideas

The third category, the situation, encompasses the conditions in which the employee performs but problems persist. Obstacles could include:

Inadequate tools or equipment to work with

Shortage of materials

Poor working conditions, including noise, distractions, inadequate lighting, lack of space, and interruptions

Unsatisfactory coworkers

Changes in methods, procedures, or equipment that create problems for the employee

Consider All Possible Solutions

A list should be made of all the possible things that can be done to improve performance. These should be listed under the categories of what the employee can do, what the manager can do, and what situations should be changed.

On the basis of extensive research concerning the growth and development of managers, Norman Allhiser, of the Management Institute at University of Wisconsin—Extension, identified some job-related growth activities. These are the results of his research, listed in order from most effective to least effective:

Attendance at staff meetings

Job rotation

Discussions with staff specialists

Study of manuals and procedure guides

Attendance at technical department programs

Temporary assignments to other departments

Allhiser found that the example set by the manager was the single most important factor in the growth and development of employees.

These are possible approaches to consider when preparing the performance improvement plan. Off-the-job activities are also important ingredients of a performance improvement plan. The most common options are attending programs, reading books and articles, and participating actively in professional and/or trade organizations.

Following are sample lists of possible actions for improving performance in orienting and training new employees, jointly developed in interviews between Anna Severson, the manager, and Christopher Green, the employee (a supervisor). After the lists, we present the final performance improvement plan that was developed from them.

Possible Actions by Christopher Green
1. Talk with another supervisor who does an effective job of orienting and training new employees.
2. Observe that supervisor when she orients and trains a new employee.
3. Attend the orientation meeting conducted by the human resources department with new employees.
4. Determine the best time for new employees to come into the department.
5. Set aside sufficient time to orient and train each new employee.
6. Have an "expert" observe the next time Christopher orients and trains a new employee. Have the "expert" critique and offer suggestions.
7. Attend a seminar on orienting and training employees.
8. Read books on the subject.

Possible Actions by Anna Severson
1. Talk with each of Christopher's new employees at the end of the first week of employment to find out how they are doing and how they feel about their jobs. Look for indications of good and bad things that happened in their orientation and training. Discuss this information with Christopher.
2. Be sure that no special pressure or assignments are given Christopher to prevent him from doing an effective job of orienting and training new employees.
3. Work with human resources department to be sure that new em-

ployees are sent to Christopher's department when he wants them to come.

4. Suggest the name of an effective trainer for Christopher to talk with and watch.

5. Correct any of the situations that hinder or prevent Christopher from doing an effective job.

6. Find an expert (possibly from the human resources or training department) to observe Christopher the next time he orients and trains a new employee.

7. Find out what training courses are available that Christopher might attend.

8. Find out the names of specific books that Christopher can read to learn about effective ways to train new employees.

Possible Situations to Be Corrected

1. New employees will come to Christopher's department when it is most convenient for Christopher.

2. A quiet office will be provided for Christopher so that he can spend time talking with and orienting each new employee.

3. A special place will be set aside for training new employees. No employee will be placed into a production situation until the training has been completed.

Finalize the Plan

The preceding list of possible actions does not constitute a plan. It must be converted into specifics of what will be done, by whom, and when.

Figure 4-1 shows the specific plan that Christopher and Anna worked out together. Larry Jackson, the training director, assisted. This performance improvement plan meets the requirements that it be practical, specific, and time oriented. It spells out what each person will do and by when. Most important, both Christopher and Anna are committed to it.

The Dayton-Hudson Approach

Dayton-Hudson Corporation developed a practical approach to individualized development, under the leadership of Paul Chaddock, vice president of organization planning and development. The feedback from the operating companies that have used this approach has been very positive.

Figure 4-1. Performance improvement plan.

Employee: Christopher Green, Supervisor
Manager: Anna Severson, Department Head
Date: October 1
Performance to Be Improved: Orienting and Training New Employees

Action to Be Taken	By Whom	When
1. Talk with Nancy Taylor about her approach.	Christopher Green	October 15
2. Watch Nancy Taylor when she orients and trains a new employee.	Christopher Green	The next time she does it
3. Attend new employee orientation meeting conducted by personnel department.	Christopher Green	The next time it is done
4. Decide on the best time for new employees to come to the department.	Christopher Green working with personnel department	By October 20
5. Attend a seminar on "How to Train New Employees."	Christopher Green	November 15 University of Wisconsin—Extension, Milwaukee
6. Read the following books: a. *Self-Development for Supervisors and Managers,* by Norman Allhiser b. *No-Nonsense Communication,* by Donald Kirkpatrick c. *The Supervisor an On-the-Job Training,* by Martin Broadwell	Christopher Green	 by October 15 by November 10 by December 12
7. Observe Christopher Green orienting and training a new employee.	Larry Jackson, Training Director	The next time Christopher Green trains a new employee
8. Talk with Christopher Green's next three new employees.	Anna Severson	One week after hire
9. Provide a check list to Christopher Green for orienting new employees.	Larry Jackson	October 15
10. Arrange for a special office for Christopher Green to use when orienting each new employee.	Anna Severson	October 15
11. Arrange for a permanent special training place for new employees.	Anna Severson	January 1

A booklet called "Individual Development Plan" (IDP) was developed as an aid for managers.[1] It had two purposes: To help employees improve performance on present jobs, and to help employees with future potential to prepare for possible promotion through a preplanned series of learning activities. Emphasis was placed on improving present job performance.

The IDP grows directly out of performance reviews. Figure 4-2 shows the relationship between performance and the plan and is designed to improve performance on the present job. It is used to help a person overcome weaknesses and build on strengths. Figure 4-3 shows the form used when a person is preparing for promotion.

The specific plan for performance improvement at Dayton-Hudson uses three different kinds of resources, as illustrated in Figure 4-4: outside sources, intraorganizational activities, and personal self-regulatory activities.

Figure 4-5 shows an example of a completed form aimed at improving an employee's management of time. Emphasis is placed on intra-

Figure 4-2. IDP form for improving performance on the present job.

Things to Change	Individual Development Plan	Done
Position responsibilities not achieved during the past twelve months, or areas of weakness:		
Individual strengths to build on:		

Figure 4-3. IDP form for preparing for promition.

Positions to which you aspire:	Steps to take to get ready:	Done

Figure 4-4. IDP form for ideas for an individual development plan.

Performance Area to Improve: _____		
From Outside Sources	Interorganizational Activities	Personal Self-Regulatory Activities

organizational activities and personal self-regulatory activities. A manager and employee working together can do more to produce growth than any other force inside or outside the organization.

The Secondary Performance Improvement Plan

We have emphasized that a plan should be developed to cover only *one* area to improve. This is important to be sure that improvement will take place in at least one part of the job. It was also suggested that three areas to improve be identified, along with three areas of strengths. This means that when one performance improvement plan has been implemented wholly or at least partially, a new plan should be developed for a second area that needs improvement. If the plans aren't too complicated, manager and employee can work on more than one performance improvement plan at a time.

The Manager and the Performance Improvement Plan

When any type of plan is developed between manager and employee, the manager automatically assumes the final responsibility for the implementation of the plan. This responsibility falls into five practical steps:

1. Be sure the employee understands the plan that was developed. The joint development of the plan almost ensures this. Both manager and employee get a copy of the plan.

Figure 4-5. Completed IDP form for improving time management.

Performance Area to Improve: Time Management		
From Outside Sources	Interorganizational Activities	Personal Self-Regulatory Activities
(To be done by employee) Read Lakein's book *How To Get Control of Your Time and Your Life.* Attend a time management workshop.	(To be done by manager) Set up interview with or assign subordinate to a task force led by a skilled time manager. Every day for one week, show your employee how you schedule and manage your own time. Ask to see the "To Do" and "Deadlines Made or Missed" lists that you assign this employee. Reinforce every single indication of effective time management.	(To be done by employee) Interview a manager who spends time wisely, and select two or three practices to adopt for yourself. Make daily "To Do" lists, and set priorities for all items. Keep a written record of your completion score. Supplement your "To Do" list with projected time allocations for each task. Keep written records of deadlines made or missed. Refuse to allow yourself to stay overtime or come in early as a way to bail yourself out of your backlogs. Review your calender for the past three months. Identify activities that were unnecessary or that used an inappropriate amount of time. Then plan your next month to correct those situations.

2. Discuss a change in plan if any circumstances occur to warrant it. Make changes on the written plan.
3. Periodically, remind the employee of commitments before their due date. This helps the employee to meet the due dates and prevents failures because of forgetting.
4. Provide continuous help in the implementation of the plan. At the time of a reminder, the manager can ask, "Do you see any problems in meeting the deadline? Can I help you in any way?"
5. Correct the employee if certain parts of the plan are not met on schedule. It has been suggested above that prevention is much better than cure. But if a failure occurs, the manager must see that the situation is corrected and the employee gets back on schedule.

The problem is to accomplish these five steps without causing resentment. The solution depends on the rapport that is maintained between manager and employee. If the tone is kept positive and the manager controls her emotions, there is a very good chance that the plan will be implemented on schedule and everyone will be happy.

The Employee and the Performance Improvement Plan

The agreement on the performance improvement plan is the beginning of the on-the-job coaching. The manager immediately picks up an obligation to see that the plan is carried out. Likewise, the employee picks up an obligation to implement the plan or to let the manager know as soon as anything happens that makes the plan impractical. When a plan becomes unrealistic, a revision in the plan is just as necessary as a revision in a standard when the standard is no longer appropriate. If something comes up that makes it impossible or impractical to carry out any phase of the plan, the employee must realize that it is her responsibility to call it to the attention of the manager.

Summary

A specific written performance improvement plan is very helpful toward improving performance. This plan should include what will be done, by whom, and when.

To be effective the plan should be practical, time oriented, and specific, with commitment on the part of both manager and employee. The best way to accomplish these four requirements is for manager and employee to develop it together. A training professional, if available, can provide valuable assistance.

A good approach is to identify three specific kinds of actions to be taken: what will be done by the employee, what will be done by the manager, and what situations or conditions will be changed. The implementation of the plan becomes the joint responsibility of manager and employee, with the manager playing the role of coach.

Note

1. Dayton-Hudson Corporation, "Individual Development Plan," Minneapolis, 1979.

CHAPTER 5

On-the-Job Coaching

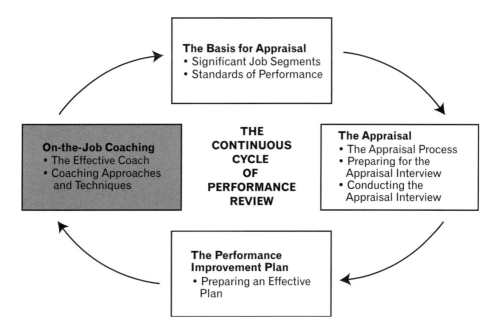

The Basis for Appraisal
- Significant Job Segments
- Standards of Performance

On-the-Job Coaching
- The Effective Coach
- Coaching Approaches and Techniques

THE CONTINUOUS CYCLE OF PERFORMANCE REVIEW

The Appraisal
- The Appraisal Process
- Preparing for the Appraisal Interview
- Conducting the Appraisal Interview

The Performance Improvement Plan
- Preparing an Effective Plan

The Effective Coach

As soon as the word "coach" is mentioned, thoughts turn to athletics. And different coaches come to mind. People begin to identify effective coaches and analyze why they were successful, and the arguments begin as to who was the best and what characteristics and approaches are most effective.

What Makes a Good Coach?

What are the characteristics of an effective coach? Do these characteristics apply only to athletic coaches, or do they apply to managers as "coaches" in industry, business, and government? To answer these questions, I wrote letters to some well-known coaches and asked them this question: "What are the characteristics (qualities, approaches, and so on) of an effective coach?" Here are the replies I received.

Barry Alvarez, athletic director and head football coach, University of Wisconsin:

> An effective coach maximizes and utilizes the abilities of his players.

Bobby Bowden, head football coach, Florida State University:

> For one thing, we know that "looks" and body build have nothing to do with the characteristics of an effective coach. The first characteristic is that the coach must have the ability to communicate. If he can't, he won't succeed. I don't mean he has to have full command of English vocabulary, but he must be able to teach and be understood.
>
> Second, the coach must have integrity, or, in simpler terms, be totally honest with everyone. Once trust breaks down because of falsehoods, the coach's decline will begin.
>
> Third, the coach needs to show compassion. He really must love those under him as well as those over him. A coach can be a dictator and show no compassion for players or employees, but I feel his days will be numbered. A coach can't treat everyone the same but must be fair.
>
> Fourth and last, the coach must have courage of his convictions. He must set the program up—its parameters, rules and regulations, discipline points, press relations, and so on, and stick to them. A coach can be flexible but not at the cost of ideals.

J. Frank Broyles, former director of athletics, University of Arkansas:

> In my opinion, an effective coach should be a living example of the virtues he teaches.

Paul F. Dietzel, former director of athletics, Louisiana State University:

> It is extremely important that the coach have a fine technical knowledge of the sport he or she is attempting to coach. That is third in

line of importance. The second most important thing is how hard this coach works at the profession. How hard you work at your profession shows when no one is watching you. However, the single most important ingredient is the loyalty the coach displays to his fellow coaches, to his team, and to the organization that he represents. In other words, does the coach have a genuine "like" for the people he or she coaches and an abiding interest in them after they are no longer able to participate for that coach? Maybe that could be spelled out in another way: "Do you really want to be of service to young people?" Whatever it is, that ingredient—a genuine concern for the athlete—has to be of number one importance.

John Erickson, former president of the Fellowship of Christian Athletes; former head basketball coach, University of Wisconsin; former general manager, Milwaukee Bucks:

I have always thought that to be effective, a coach must be an excellent teacher and a person with leadership qualities. These two general but important characteristics include more specific requirements such as:

1. Solid knowledge of what one is teaching.
2. Good motivation skills as well as effective communication.
3. A deep personal concern for each team member.
4. Ability to make decisions under pressure and live with these decisions without second-guessing oneself.
5. Willingness to confess mistakes and build on the experience.
6. Complete honesty in all situations.
7. Willingness to be an example for players in all areas of life.
8. Ability to keep all things in perspective, recognizing priorities of life—God, family, others, and my work.

Elroy Hirsch, former director of athletics, University of Wisconsin:

I firmly believe that you cannot put a coach into a mold. In other words, I feel that successful coaches are different in their makeup and their tactics. For instance, John McKay, a loose, even-going coach with a great sense of humor, is far different from a Bo Schembechler or a Woody Hayes. Likewise, Dave McClain is far different from a Bear Bryant. One thing all these people do have in common, however, is their dedication to the job—that is, they know no bounds on the hours they work, there are no days in the week—they are totally dedicated to the work at hand. Through their individual personalities they conquer the job before them.

If the coach has other qualities, so much the better. In other words, he should be very good on his feet, be able to meet the public well, be friendly and warm to one and all. Many times this is very, very difficult in the face of criticism from alumni, fans, and so on. He must have patience with young people, for it is his job to teach as well as to coach. He must be a very strong supervisor, for his assistant coaches must do his every bidding and do the job properly. Along this line, the selection of his staff is most important. He must not be afraid of having very sound, good people around him. He must not be afraid that someone underneath him is trying to take over his job. He must surround himself with strength, and of course this requires him to be an effective manager of personnel.

To a somewhat lesser degree, he must also understand the budgetary process. It is very easy to give a coach a free hand and let him spend all the money he wishes to accomplish the job; however, in our situation and in most situations in intercollegiate athletics, we are restricted by budget limitations, and the coach must understand the budget process and live within those limitations.

What we, in effect, are looking for is a "perfect man." It is very difficult to find one that possesses all the qualities for the ideal coach, but we try to come as close to it as possible. The structure of intercollegiate athletics is wrong in my estimation . . . in effect we are telling our income-sport coaches . . . who generate nearly all of the income which supports the entire 27-sports programs . . . , "If you are not successful, and if you don't draw large crowds and generate large amounts of income, we are going to fire you." I think that is totally unfair. However, this is part of the pressure that the head coach in the income-producing sports must work under.

Mike Holder, golf coach, Oklahoma State University:

He listens to his players and lets them tell how to make them better. Their comments include: Leave me alone; I don't respond well to pressure; I like it when you walk with me on the golf course; you say nicer things to me than I say to myself.

Bob Knight, head basketball coach, Texas Tech:

> The most important characteristic, I think, that an effective coach must have is the ability to make decisions. This applies not only to what transpires on the court or around basketball but on a day-to-day involvement he has with his program. I have long felt that the most important thing that a coach can teach is discipline. Discipline to me is doing something when it has to be done, as well as it can be done, and doing it that way all the time.

Mike Krzyzewski, head basketball coach, Duke University:

> The ability to communicate and be completely trustworthy are the two main characteristics of an effective coach. Upon these characteristics, a strong relationship can develop.

Tom Landry, former head football coach, Dallas Cowboys:

> An effective athletic coach must be a teacher, a psychologist, and a motivator. He must possess leadership qualities, and at the same time, he needs the confidence and concentration to operate at maximum efficiency under great stress.

Joanne P. McCallie, head women's basketball coach, Michigan State University:

> Effective coaches communicate consistently, directly, and fairly, while understanding each individual player's experience, background, family, abilities, goals, and dreams. It is an ever-changing process that involves the ability to develop people daily.

Al McGuire, former head basketball coach, Marquette University:

> A good coach is a person that stands the test of time. He uses team plays the same exact way the last five minutes of the game as the first five. He is also a person that has no other outside interest. They are usually guys that are not interested in having smoke rings blowing at them and are not continually trying to make supplemental income.

Ray Meyer, former head basketball coach, DePaul University:

> I believe a coach has to put the sport in its proper perspective. It is a game, and one's life does not depend upon it. When he understands this, he coaches without putting extra pressure on the players. They will play freer and better. A coach must have patience. He can't expect too much too soon. He is a teacher. Probably the greatest quality a coach can have is understanding. He must understand that each player is an individual and must be treated as such. All players cannot be treated alike. Some you can improve by loud criticism, and others need encouragement. No coach can treat all players alike, for each one is an individual.

Tom Osborne, former head football coach, University of Nebraska:

> I believe that the qualities of an effective coach are good organizational skills, a capacity to work long hours, an ability to communicate effectively with his athletes, an ability to maintain composure and to think clearly in pressure situations, and an ability to communicate a genuine sense of concern for the general well-being of his players.

Ara Parseghian, former head football coach, Notre Dame University:

> Defining the characteristics of an effective coach is not easily done. In responding, a series of words came to mind . . . , and I won't attempt to weigh them. Here are some of the words that have crossed my mind.

> | | |
> |---|---|
> | Dedicated | Communicator |
> | Confident | Enthusiastic |
> | Consistent | Disciplinarian |
> | Hard-working | Perseverance |
> | Leader | Strategically abreast of trends |
> | Loyal | Articulate |
> | Honest | Flexible |
> | Knowledgeable | Humble |

> I guess the last man that had these qualities, they put on the Cross.

Joseph Paterno, head football coach, The Pennsylvania State University:

An effective athletic coach must possess sound moral values and the ability to relate to all types of people. He must be dedicated, loyal, and sincere about his beliefs and philosophies and must be willing to accept success and failure as part of the game. Above and beyond all things he must have a true love for the sport and at all times realize the responsibility he has to his players.

Richard "Digger" Phelps, former head basketball coach, University of Notre Dame:

My advice would be to know the game and be ready to make adjustments. But, most importantly, a coach must always be himself.

Kevin Sampson, head basketball coach, University of Oklahoma:

An effective coach establishes a relationship built on trust and respect. It is hard to coach a kid if he doesn't think you care about him.

Bill Self, head basketball coach, University of Kansas:

The important characteristics of a coach can be broken down into five categories: Comprehension, Outlook, Character, Humor, and Affection.

Comprehension
- Rules.
- Skills.
- Tactics required.
- Long-term plans for individual improvement during the season and off season.
- Staying in contact with various basketball-related organizations to keep learning and refreshing mental aspects of coaching.
- Variety of drills to use for developing basketball skills.
- Putting your student athletes in positions where they have to develop socially.
- Being able to implement proper training.

Outlook

- Goals and perspectives of what you want or seeking as coach.
- Common objectives.
- Help players develop physically, mentally, and socially to become better players and people.
- Enjoyable experience.
- To win in your sport and in life!

Character

- Modeling appropriate behaviors for sport and life—more than just saying the right things.
- What you say and what you do must match.
- Challenge, support, encourage, reward every student athletic and your players will be more likely to accept—even celebrate—their differences.
- Be in control—before, during, and after games and practices.
- Don't be afraid to admit when you are wrong—no one is perfect.
- Your words and actions should show your student athletes that every individual matters and therefore you will be teaching them a valuable lesson about respecting and supporting individual differences.
- On a personal note: Be aware of your strengths and weaknesses—try to build on your strengths.

Humor

- An often overlooked coaching tool.
- Having the ability to laugh at yourself and with the players at practices and games if the situation calls for it.
- Sense of humor—puts in perspective the many mistakes our young student athletes will make.
- Don't get upset at each mistake.
- Allow your players and yourself to enjoy the ups and learn from the downs.
- Consider laughter by your players a sign of enjoyment—provided they are paying attention.

Affection

- A vital tool you want to have in your coaching demeanor.
- Genuine concern for the individual athletes and the young people you coach and teach.

- A desire to show them your love and knowledge of your respected sport.
- Patience and understanding that allows each individual playing for you to grow from his or her involvement playing the sport.
- A real concern for the health and welfare of the student athletes.
- Recognize the similarities between people's sport experiences and other activities of their lives—and encourage to strive to learn from all of their experiences—to become a well-rounded individual.
- Show a desire to work with student athletes and be involved in their personal growth as a person and athlete.
- Patience to work with those who are slower to learn or who are less capable to perform.

Dean E. Smith, former head basketball coach, University of North Carolina:

1. The coach should care about the people under his guidance.
2. He should decide how best to use his personnel and then have the ability to teach.
3. It is important to motivate each individual to work to the best of his ability.

Orlando "Tubby" Smith, head basketball coach, University of Kentucky:

I believe a coach has to be willing to serve. He should provide leadership and guidance for his players, staff, fans, University, for the entire athletic department, particularly the basketball community where he coaches and lives. My responsibility is to help each individual to reach his potential and dreams. When I am a servant to others, I am an effective coach.

Bill Snyder, head football coach, Kansas State University:

1. Understand that which highly and positively motivates those you are leading/coaching.
2. Genuinely care about those you lead/coach.
3. Set the example.

4. Expect and demand a great deal of yourself first, then others. Display and demand discipline.
5. Provide fair and equitable responsibility and accountability.
6. Display and expect loyalty, honesty, and trust.
7. Have a strong belief in "your system." Know exactly what you need to achieve, and develop a well-thought-out plan to achieve it. And, get everyone on board with the goal and the plan.

Bart Starr, former head football coach, Green Bay Packers:

To begin, I believe he is goal oriented and has a plan by which to accomplish those goals and a method by which to measure progress along the way. Additionally, he is extremely self-confident, very poised, has the ability to accept criticism, and receive coaching himself, has a strong faith in God, and a good sense of humor. Further, I think that all successful coaches tend to be so because they operate within their own personality and framework.

Roy Williams, head basketball coach, University of North Carolina:

The program must be based on players and coaches with character. Everyone must be willing to make sacrifices for the team. There must be trust from coach to player and player to coach. No personal agenda or goal can be bigger than the team agenda. The coach's goals should always be more important than the problems. The coach must take care of little things and keep focused on the target.
   My favorite quotes are:

1. Everyone has the will to win—champions have the will to prepare.
2. Good teams have good players—*great* teams have *great* teammates.
3. Be led by your dreams—not pushed by your problems.

It's amazing how much can be accomplished when no one cares who gets the credit!

John Wooden, former head basketball coach, UCLA:

These are the essential personal traits and abilities for a coach:

Primary Traits	Secondary Traits
Industriousness	Affability
Enthusiasm	Appearance
Sympathy	Voice
Judgment	Adaptability
Self-control	Cooperativeness
Earnestness	Forcefulness
Patience	Accuracy
Attentiveness to detail	Alertness
Impartiality	Reliability
Integrity	Optimism
Organizational skills	Resourcefulness
Self-discipline	Vision

A coach must communicate with those under his supervision; listen and not be disagreeable when there is disagreement; keep in mind that the goal of criticism is to improve, prevent, correct, or help and not to punish; make those under his supervision feel that they are working with him rather than for him; be more interested in finding the best way than in having his own way; be well organized and not waste time; and be genuinely concerned about his players.

In his book *They Call Me Coach,* Wooden adds:

No coach should be trusted with the tremendous responsibility of handling young men under the great mental, emotional, and physical strain to which they are subjected unless he is spiritually strong. If he does possess this inner strength, it is only because he has faith and truly loves his fellow man. This was the belief of Amos Alonzo Stagg, who also felt that the obligations, opportunities and responsibilities in coaching are manifold. The coach who is committed to the Christlike life will be helping youngsters under his supervision to develop wholesome disciplines of body, mind, and spirit that will build character worthy of his Master's calling. He must set the proper example by word and by deed.[1]

I also asked Jon McGlocklin, former basketball star with Indiana University and the Milwaukee Bucks, what he thought were the qualities of an effective coach. He replied:

I feel that a successful coach must possess the ability to communicate and relate to his players as people and athletes. He must be disciplined and command the respect of his players. He must be knowledgeable in his sport and yet capable of admitting a mistake. And, finally, it helps to have talented players if winning is everything! If not, he builds his players as athletes and men.

A Composite Image of the Ideal Coach

If we piece together the different comments of these well-known and successful coaches, a picture of the ideal coach begins to emerge. He has knowledge—of the players, the game, and finance and budgets. He has skills and abilities in many areas, including these:

Recruiting players and staff of assistants
Establishing goals and objectives
Planning and organization
Communication
Motivating each person as an individual
Teaching
Correcting and criticizing without causing resentment
Making decisions
Listening
Discipline
Measuring performance and progress toward goals
Finding the best way, which is not necessarily the coach's way
Establishing and executing proper priorities
Operating effectively under stress
Relating to all types of people

The ideal coach has the following personal qualities:

Enthusiasm and dedication	Self-confidence
Self-control	Humility
Patience	Perseverence
Impartiality	Genuine concern for players
Integrity and honesty	Warmth
Friendliness	Willingness to admit mistakes
Optimism	Willingness to accept criticism
Resourcefulness	Sense of humor
Vision	Flexibility
Forcefulness	Love of the sport

Consistency   Willingness to accept success
Being part of the team   and failure as part of the game
Open-mindedness   Strong sense of moral values

Finally, a good coach sets an example. Frank Broyles and John Erickson both emphasize that the coach must be a living example for the players. John Wooden quotes this poem to illustrate the importance of this:

A careful man I ought to be, a little fellow follows me.
I do not dare to go astray for fear he'll go the self-same way.

Not once can I escape his eyes, what e'er he sees me do, he tries.
Like me he says he's going to be, the little chap who follows me.

I must remember as I go through summer sun and winter snow,
I'm building for the years to be, that little chap who follows me.

The Manager as "Coach"

The manager in industry, business, and government is a person who supervises a number of employees. Her situation is almost identical to that of the athletic coach in many ways.

First of all, the manager must get the best effort and performance from each employee and is constantly trying to help employees improve, both for their own benefit and for that of the organization.

In many situations, the manager is concerned with a team of workers, as well as with the performance of each individual worker. This is similar to the situation of coaches of team sports like basketball, football, and hockey. Other times, the manager is primarily concerned with individual workers because each person pretty much works alone, as in sports like swimming, track, tennis, and golf.

If employees performing under a manager don't like the situation, they have available options such as letting up on performance, complaining, causing dissension among the other workers, and quitting. Athletes can do all these things, too.

Managers have some employees who are better than others and who therefore receive higher rewards than others. Sometimes the employees make more money than the manager does.

Managers are under constant pressure to produce with the people and resources available. Sometimes, accidents, sickness, and other problems reduce these resources. Like coaches, managers are concerned about competition. In order to stay in business, they must meet or beat the competition—with whatever resources, they *do* have.

Finally, managers have the same opportunities to give rewards that coaches have, and they face the same limitations. Most managers are limited in how much money they can give, but they have ample opportunities to give nonfinancial rewards such as praise, additional responsibility, additional freedom, and special job assignments and to solicit team members' ideas.

According to Florence M. Stone, the author of the book *Coaching, Counseling, and Mentoring*, the duties of a manager as coach are the following:

- To act as a role model for higher performance
- To hire the best
- To create a work environment in which employees have reason to be motivated
- To clarify expectations—both micro expectations associated with particular jobs and macro objectives tied to the organization's overall strategy and mission
- To provide feedback on your employees' behavior that will put them on the right track and keep them there
- To apply the performance evaluation process not only as a measurement tool tied to raises but also as a developmental aid
- To provide the training and resources employees need to improve their performance
- To praise, praise, and praise some more to reinforce positive performance[2]

Summary

Because the job of a manager is very similar to the job of an athletic coach, many of the characteristics of an effective athletic coach also are those of a good manager. Just as athletic coaches have different types of players to work with, managers have employees with differences in attitudes, knowledge, and skills. In both situations, the challenge is to mold people into an effective team to accomplish the goals of the organization and to help employees accomplish their own goals at the same time.

Coaching Approaches and Techniques

The terms "coaching" and "counseling" are frequently used to describe the on-the-job conversations that take place between manager and employee. Some organizations use the words interchangeably to mean the same thing. Others differentiate between the two words. In this book, the word "coaching" has a different meaning from "counseling." Here are the characteristics of each:

Counseling

1. The employee usually initiates discussion.
2. Counseling takes place when a problem arises or when the employee feels a problem needs solving.
3. The problem can be personal or job oriented.
4. Emphasis is on listening on the part of the manager.
5. The manager avoids giving specific advice and helps the employee solve his or her own problem.
6. The objectives are to solve a specific problem and/or to relieve tension on the part of the employee.

Coaching

1. The manager usually initiates discussion.
2. It is done on a regular basis.
3. It is job oriented.
4. It is positive or corrective, with emphasis on telling, training, and teaching by the manager.
5. The manager frequently gives specific advice on what to do and how to do it.
6. The objective is to improve the job performance of the employee as an individual and a team member.

What Coaching Is Not

Managerial coaching is *not* a specific set of instructions that a manager has developed about activities or behavior of the employee. It is *not* a set of tasks to be performed with demands for vaguely determined outcomes such as "hitting the ball." And it is *not* some action or policy that inhibits movement, requires sitting overly long in one position, or extols the virtues of patience and humility.

The following examples represent what is often the bulk of the activities of the manager who imagines that he or she is coaching employees:

- The plant manager who daily calls her staff together and pours forth wisdom about the mistakes of the day before, with somber warnings of "Let's watch that one," is seriously attempting to coach but is lamentably ineffective at it.
- The sales manager who uses staff meetings to divulge deep insights about top-management goals and thinking, in the form of ten-minute speeches, is often doing nothing more than using communication as a club to beat down any incipient new ideas or change from employees.
- The staff manager who counterpunches with employees, insisting that they produce new ideas but shooting these full of holes when they appear, may be utterly sincere but is also utterly incompetent in coaching.

What Coaching Is

The effective coaching function is more apt to take the form of working on forward-looking plans and objectives for employees in a way that keeps them moving constantly toward new areas of experience, new demands for personal skill development, and application of ingenuity and problem solving. On-the-job coaching improves job performance in two ways, and the principles and approaches involved are the same for both. First, day-to-day coaching takes place whenever the need arises, and it bolsters the relationship between the manager and the employee. If an employee makes a mistake, the manager helps the employee correct it, and this coaching should prevent the same mistake from happening again. If, on the other hand, the employee does an especially good job, the manager compliments the employee. This is also part of the coaching process.

The other reason for coaching is to help the employee implement the performance improvement plan that was developed as part of the performance review program. The manager should periodically see how the employee is progressing and provide help in implementing the plan.

Day-to-Day Coaching

The manager must play a day-to-day coaching role, which is based on observing the performance of the employee. If the employee performs well, the manager provides positive reinforcement. If the employee fails to so something that should be done, the manager calls it to the attention of the employee to find out why it wasn't done and to see that it is done. Or the employee may do something that should not be done. This requires the manager to find out the reason for the mistake and to take whatever action is appropriate.

The key to effective coaching is to handle problem situations without causing resentment on the part of the employee. Resentment can easily be created by an eager coach who is overly anxious to correct an error. For example, a direct approach to pointing out the mistake and an order to the employee to do it right could well cause resentment. To avoid resentment, a tactful approach is usually required.

If the manager sees an employee making a mistake, there are four possible courses of action to take:

1. Ignore the situation and hope that the employee will see the mistake and correct it.
2. Call immediate attention to the mistake and ask the employee to do the right thing.
3. Use an indirect approach such as, "How are things going?" If the employee knows about the mistake, she may frankly admit the mistake and tell the manager, "Don't worry. I'll take care of it." If the employee doesn't realize that a mistake has been made, the answer might be, "Fine. No problems!" In this case the manager will have to call attention to the mistake and ask, "What can we do to correct it?"
4. Use the "sandwich" approach. This means to praise the subordinate for good work, call attention to the mistake, and end up with a positive statement such as, "I'm sure that this won't happen again."

Some people ridicule the fourth approach by saying that the employee will recognize the technique and after the first words of praise will immediately react, "O.K., what have I done wrong?" Obviously, the success or failure of the "sandwich" technique depends on the frequency of its use. If the only time a manager praises a employee is to provide the first part of the "sandwich," the approach will backfire. But if praise is regularly used by the manager to recognize good work, the technique can be successful. In any case, it must be remembered that praise is recognizing good work that has actually been done, not just using complimentary words when they aren't true. As Wooden said, "I try to follow any criticism with a pat on the back, realizing that I cannot antagonize and influence at the same time."[3]

Among these four choices for correcting poor work, there is no guarantee that any will be successful or unsuccessful. For example, if the manager uses the first approach (doesn't say anything), the employee may not recognize the mistake and correct it. Likewise, the "sandwich" method may be successful with one employee and unsuccessful with another.

The important point is that the coaching must be done to correct the situation—now and in the future—and not to cause resentment. It's like a prisoner who goes to jail. After paying for the crime, the prisoner may come out with an attitude that says, "I've learned a lesson. Next time I won't get caught!" Or the prisoner may come out with an attitude that says, "I've learned my lesson. I won't do it again." Obviously, the second result is the one to seek from employees as well as prisoners. Here are some specific suggestions that will help you achieve this.

If the employee has done a good job, the manager has a very pleasant situation. Positive reinforcement should be offered immediately. If there are other people within hearing distance, so much the better. They realize that the employee has done something well, and they are pleased to see a manager recognize it. Obviously, they hope to be treated the same way when they do something worthy of praise. Even if the performance wasn't perfect, a compliment can be sincerely given to recognize improvement. And complimenting improvement generally leads to continued effort by the employee and better results in the future.

Some managers compliment warmly when a job is well done. Others ignore it and act as if they thought, "That's what we are paying you for; why should I have to tell you, besides?"

In sporting events, some coaches do not give praise when a player does an exceptionally good job. Other coaches openly show signs of enthusiasm and give praise for good work. Ara Parseghian is an example of the latter type of coach. When he was head football coach at Notre Dame and a player made an exceptionally good play, Ara would jump up and down, give his player a hug or pat on the back, and pay him a nice compliment like "Good play!" That spirit and outward expression brought out the best in his players.

If the employee has done a poor job, the coach should usually correct a situation as soon as it occurs. Sometimes, however, this isn't a good idea because it might not be the right time and place. For example, there may be other people around when the employee has made a mistake. Also, the coach may be emotionally upset. In these situations, it is important to correct the employee as soon as practical, but in private. One good approach might be to say, "Can I see you in my office in five minutes?" This gives the manager time to cool down and also to do a little preparation for the coaching interview. The preparation might include:

- Thinking of some good things the worker has recently done that can be mentioned.
- Trying to determine the reason why the employee made the mistake.
- Thinking how the interview should end. The employee should say or feel, "Thanks for calling this to my attention," rather than "I'll get even with you."

Dr. Earl Planty, former executive, consultant, and teacher, has some good tips for handling emotional conversations. These are listed in Table 5-1. Typical emotional situations managers must deal with involve fear, anxiety, bias, distortion, confusion, or selfish or neurotic behavior.

Table 5-1. Handling problems fraught with emotions.

Do	*Don't*
Set a supportive, quiet situation for the discussion.	Be interrupted by phone calls, coworkers, or other intrusions.
Draw off emotions; encourage release of pressure.	Interrupt.
Listen, listen, listen.	Talk too much (or the problem employee won't).
Listen to emotions, as well as facts.	Disagree.
Expect and prepare to hear negative, critical comments, and confused, distorted ones.	Correct, deny.
Restrain your own emotions in response to the other person's.	Play FBI.
Understand, empathize.	Blame.
Echo and reflect to the person the feelings expressed.	Judge.

Coaching on the Performance Improvement Plan

While day-to-day coaching takes place as needed to discuss the on-going performance of an employee, coaching regarding the performance improvement plan is a planned activity.

In Chapter 4, we presented a performance improvement plan that was jointly developed between Christopher Green, employee (supervisor), and Anna Severson, his supervisor. In this plan, Christopher agreed to do a number of things. And Anna, his manager, became his coach to ensure they would be done. The plan was developed on October 1. The first commitment was for an action by October 15, by which time Christopher agreed to talk with Nancy Taylor about her approach. Therefore, sometime before October 15, Anna should talk with Christopher to see if he has made arrangements to talk with Nancy. The same approach should be used regarding the other commitments.

Figure 5-1 is the same performance improvement plan that was described in Chapter 4, with the coaching contacts added. This is the working tool that the manager, Anna Severson, needs to be sure that effective coaching takes place. Otherwise she and Christopher may forget the details of the plan until the deadlines have gone by. By following through on the plan, Anna will emphasize to Christopher that the planning process was an important one and that it will be implemented. The coaching should be done in a very positive manner. In most cases, Anna will check with Christopher before the agreed-on date to serve as a reminder. This continues to maintain the rapport that has been built up throughout the entire performance review program. And the coaching will probably result in improved performance.

Coaching Practices of Managers

Walter Mahler conducted surveys to measure the coaching practices of managers. He divided his survey into ten major categories.[4] For each category, he asked five questions about the activities that occurred on the job, and each question had four possible answers. Typical questions were:

1. How well do you understand what is expected of you in your current position?
   _____ a. I have some idea of what is expected of me.
   _____ b. I have a fairly good idea.
   _____ c. I have a good understanding.
   _____ d. I have a very good understanding.

(text continues on page 102)

Figure 5-1. Coaching on the performance improvement plan.

Employee: Christopher Green, Supervisor Manager: Anna Severson, Department Head

Date: October 1 Performance to Be Improved: Orienting and Training New Employees

The Performance Improvement Plan			Coaching Contact by Anna Severson	
Action to Be Taken	By Whom	When	When	Results
1. Talk with Nancy Taylor about her approach.	Christopher Green	October 15	October 14	Has made arrangements to talk to Nancy tomorrow.
			October 15	Did talk with Nancy. Got some good ideas.
2. Watch Nancy Taylor when she orients and trains a new employee.	Christopher Green	The next time she does it	October 15	Nancy plans to train a new employee on November 13. Christopher will observe.
			November 15	Nancy trained a new employee and Christopher watched. Christopher felt it worthwhile.
3. Attend new employee orientation meeting conducted by personnel department.	Christopher Green	The next time it is done	October 15	Checked with personnel department and learned that it will be done November 18. Asked Christopher to be there.
			November 18	Asked Christopher for his report of the orientation meeting. He had suggestions that were passed on to personnel department.
4. Decide on the best time for new employees to come to the department.	Christopher Green working with personnel department	By October 20	October 19	Worked out the starting time for all new employees; 9 A.M. on Monday instead of 7 A.M.

(continues)

Figure 5-1. Continued.

	The Performance Improvement Plan			Coaching Contact by Anna Severson	
Action to Be Taken	By Whom	When		When	Results
5. Attend a seminar on "How to Train New Employees."	Christopher Green	November 15 University of Wisconsin—Extension, Milwaukee		November 10	Discussed program schedule and details.
				November 18	Discussed program and benefits Christopher got from it.
6. Read the following books:	Christopher Green			October 3	Arranged to order the three books Christopher has agreed to read.
a. *Self-Development for Supervisors and Managers*, by Norman Allhiser		by October 15		October 14	Learned that Christopher has read half of Allhiser's book.
b. *No-Nonsense Communication*, by Donald Kirkpatrick		by November 10		October 31	Learned that Christopher has read half of Kirkpatrick's book and all of Allhiser's.
c. *The Supervisor and On-the-Job Training*, by Martin Broadwell		by December 12		November 5	Learned that Christopher had finished Kirkpatrick and Broadwell books.
7. Observe Christopher Green orienting and training a new employee.	Larry Jackson, Training Director	The next time Christopher trains a new employee		October 20	Learned that Christopher is scheduled to hire a new employee on November 15.
				November 20	Got good feedback from Larry Jackson on Christopher's training of new employee.
8. Talk with Christopher Green's next three new employees.	Anna Severson	One week after hire		November 25	Talked with Joanne Cador, Christopher's new employee, about her start with company. Generally felt good about orientation and training. Still confused about benefits. Doesn't feel secure in her job yet.

	The Performance Improvement Plan			Coaching Contact by Anna Severson	
Action to Be Taken	By Whom	When		When	Results
9. Provide a checklist to Christopher Green for orienting new employees.	Larry Jackson	October 15		October 13	Checked with Larry Jackson on checklist. List not yet ready. Promised by October 21.
				October 21	Checked with Larry on new checklist. Not quite done.
				October 25	Checklist completed and given to Christopher.
10. Arrange for a special office for Christopher Green to use when orienting each new employee.	Anna Severson	October 15		October 10	Tried to find a special office to let Christopher use in orienting new employees. Arranged for conference room in training department when not in use. Told Christopher he could use her office if needed. Asked for twenty-four-hour notice. Will try to find another permanent place.
11. Arrange for a permanent special place for training new employees.	Anna Severson	January 1		December 1	Tried to locate a place for training new employees. Nothing available.
				December 20	Tried to locate a place for training new employees. There is a possible place in the shipping room.
				December 28	Arranged for a temporary place in a corner of shipping with temporary partitions. Will continue to try to get a permanent place.

2. How well do you know what your manager thinks of your performance (results, accomplishments)?
    _____ a. I don't know what he or she thinks of my performance.
    _____ b. I have some idea.
    _____ c. I have a good idea.
    _____ d. I have a very definite idea.
3. On the basis of the results you have secured over the past few years, do you think you have been accorded the recognition by your manager that you deserve?
    _____ a. I haven't been accorded deserved recognition.
    _____ b. Yes, I have, but with quite a few exceptions.
    _____ c. Yes, I have, with almost no exceptions.
    _____ d. I've always received the recognition I deserved.
4. How helpful has your manager been in your development and growth over the past few years?
    _____ a. He or she has helped very little.
    _____ b. He or she has helped somewhat.
    _____ c. He or she has helped considerably.
    _____ d. He or she has helped a great deal.

The results of Mahler's survey are shown in Table 5-2. For each question, the first two answers are considered unfavorable and the last are two favorable.

These results point out some serious problems related to performance appraisal and review. For example, 30 percent of the employees gave negative answers to the questions about their understanding of

Table 5-2. Coaching practices survey.

	Favorable Responses	
Factors having to do with:	Top and Middle Management*	Lower-Level Management†
Responsibilities and goals	75%	68%
Delegation	68%	62%
Knowledge of performance	58%	45%
Assistance as needed	72%	61%
Motivation	61%	46%
Working relationship	80%	82%
Benefiting from experience	50%	40%
Group activities	60%	48%
Future responsibilities	38%	32%
Coaching results	70%	65%

*From survey of 1,000 employees of 200 top and middle managers.
†From survey of 2,037 employees of 779 lower-level managers.

their responsibilities and goals. This kind of confusion is bound to have negative repercussions when appraisals are made and discussed. Even more serious is the response to the questions dealing with knowledge of performance. Nearly 50 percent of the employees who replied indicated that they didn't have a clear idea of what the manager thought of their performance. The other results point to problems that exist because of inadequate communication, appraisal, and on-the-job coaching.

Summary

This section has emphasized the two different reasons for on-the-job coaching. The first is day-to-day coaching to compliment good work and correct and improve performance that does not meet expectations and standards. The second reason for coaching is to be sure that the performance improvement plan is properly implemented. The principles and approaches for both kinds of coaching are essentially the same, and the desired results—best possible performance—are identical.

According to Mahler, managers generally do not do an effective job of coaching. Approximately 30 percent of employees surveyed do not understand their responsibilities and goals. And almost 50 percent do not know what their manager thinks of their performance. In summarizing his research, Mahler stated that less than 70 percent of managers were achieving favorable coaching results. Although this survey is twenty-five years old, it still applies to many managers today.

Notes

1. John Wooden, *They Call Me Coach* (New York: Bantam, 1973).
2. Florence M. Stone, *Coaching, Counseling and Mentoring* (New York: AMACOM, 1999).
3. Wooden.
4. Walter Mahler, "Coaching Practices Survey," unpublished paper, Midland Park, N.J., 1980.

Five Program Requirements

An Effective Performance Review Program

Up to this point, this book has focused on the specifics of a performance review program. Significant job segments and standards of performance were emphasized and described in order to clarify what is expected of an employee. The appraisal of performance was then discussed with a suggestion that a self-appraisal be included. Specific suggestions were then given on how to prepare and how to conduct an appraisal interview. The preparation of a performance improvement plan was described in detail. Chapter 5 dealt with the characteristics and techniques of an effective coach. Throughout the book, emphasis has been placed on manager and employee working together to accomplish improved performance on the part of the employee.

This chapter takes a broader view and describes the five requirements for an effective performance review program.

The Program Fits the Organization

Some programs are quite complicated and require considerable paperwork. Other programs use simple forms and procedures and keep paperwork to a minimum. Some programs require appraisals and interiews on a quarterly or semiannual basis, while others require them only annually. In choosing a program, every organization must be sure that its program can be properly implemented.

For example, a program that requires frequent appraisals and much paperwork will fail if there is a minimum of time available for those who must do the appraisals and complete the forms. It will probably also fail unless the person responsible for administering the overall program has enough time to do an effective job. Another important requirement is support from top management. Therefore, care should be taken to select a program that fits the needs, personnel, and priorities of the organization.

The Program Is Communicated

The word "communicate" means to create understanding. This means that everyone involved in the program must understand the what, why, when, where, and how. In most cases, it requires meetings to explain and discuss the program, as well as a manual that describes the forms and procedures.

I attended a recent meeting in which a manager said that his organization was using the Hay System of performance appraisal. He went on to say that those involved in the program called it the "haze system" because everyone was confused.

When introducing a new performance review program I had developed for a large corporation, the general manager of the Carlsbad plant scheduled a dinner meeting of all employees who were included in the program. Secretaries, engineers, and foremen were included, for example, even though they were not going to conduct appraisals and interviews with other employees. The general manager and I wanted to be sure they understood the program because they were going to be appraised and interviewed. In order to accomplish this communication, we prepared slides and a small booklet that supplemented the oral presentation I made. A question-and-answer session followed the presentation. By using this approach, we were confident that there would be much better understanding of the program than if we left it up to the managers to communicate the program to their employees.

The Program Is Sold

Understanding isn't enough. Those who implement the plan must be convinced that their time and effort are going to be rewarded. Initially, this can probably be done through persuasion. As time goes on, though, the benefits must be real.

When I introduced the performance review program at Carlsbad, the process of selling included the following steps:

1. Explanation of the program to the general manager, industrial relations manager, and management development supervisor. We discussed it and made some minor changes.
2. Explanation of the program to the eight department heads. We discussed it and made some changes on the basis of their recommendations.
3. Communication of the program at the dinner meeting. Benefits to the individual employees as well as to the company were stressed.
4. Individual discussion with those who weren't sold on the program.
5. Clarification by the general manager that it was *their* program and not a program that had been imposed by the corporate office. He emphasized that I had been invited to help them implement the program.

The program must be sold not just initially, but continuously. Managers constantly battle with priorities. The more they are sold on the program, the more likely they are to give time and energy to it and do it effectively.

The Reviewers Are Trained

It's not enough to create understanding and sell the managers on the program. They must have the necessary skills to implement the program. To get them to understand the forms and procedures is relatively easy, but to get them to develop the required skills is difficult. And a well-written manual isn't going to do it.

With our program, the necessary skills were:

Identifying significant job segments
Developing standards of performance
Appraising performance
Conducting the appraisal interview
Developing a performance improvement plan
Coaching

All these skills required practice. So we established a training program as follows:

FIRST MEETING (2 hours)

Objectives	1. Understand the performance review program. 2. Learn how to identify significant job segments.
Agenda	1. Overview of the program. 2. Description of significant job segments. 3. Examples of significant job segments. 4. Each person lists significant job segments for his or her own job.
Assignment	Get together with one of your employees and jointly develop significant job segments for her job.

SECOND MEETING (3 hours)

Objectives	1. Review significant job segments. 2. Learn how to write standards of performance.
Agenda	1. Discussion of significant job segments that were developed as an assignment. 2. Meaning of standards of performance. 3. Characteristics of standards of performance. 4. Examples of standards of performance. 5. Each person writes one standard of performance.
Assignment	Jointly develop with the employee standards of performance for *one* of the significant job segments from the previous assignment.

THIRD MEETING (2 hours)

Objectives	1. Review standards of performance. 2. Understand appraisal by the supervisor. 3. Understand self-appraisal. 4. Learn how to complete appraisal form.
Agenda	1. Discussion of standards of performance that had been developed as an assignment. 2. Explanation of the appraisal process. 3. Explanation of the appraisal form. 4. Samples of completed appraisal forms. 5. Each person completes a sample appraisal form.

Assignment   1. Complete an appraisal form on the employee.
                  2. Get the employee to complete the self-appraisal form.

FOURTH MEETING (3 hours)

Objectives   1. Review the appraisal process and forms.
                  2. Understand guidelines for an effective appraisal interview.
                  3. Learn how to conduct an appraisal interview.

Agenda   1. Discussion of completed appraisal forms from the assignment.
                  2. Explanation of guidelines for an effective appraisal interview.
                  3. Demonstration of a poor appraisal interview.
                  4. Demonstration of a good appraisal interview.
                  5. In groups of three, each person in turn takes the role of interviewer, interviewee, and observer. The observer leads the critique after each practice interview.

Assignment   Conduct an appraisal interview with the employee.

FIFTH MEETING (2 hours)

Objectives   1. Review the appraisal interview.
                  2. Understand a performance improvement plan.
                  3. Learn to prepare a performance improvement plan.

Agenda   1. Discussion of the appraisal interview completed as an assignment.
                  2. Explanation of a performance improvement plan.
                  3. Examples of a performance improvement plan.
                  4. Each person writes a performance improvement plan.

Assignment   Jointly develop with employee a performance improvement plan for one aspect of the job.

SIXTH MEETING (2 hours)

Objectives   1. Review the performance improvement plan.
                  2. Understand on-the-job coaching.
                  3. Review the entire performance review program.

Agenda
1. Discussion of the performance improvement plan that was developed as an assignment.
2. Explanation of characteristics of an effective coach.
3. Explanation of coaching techniques.
4. Review of the entire program.

The length of the six training meetings (two or three hours each) was established to accomplish the objective. The amount of time between sessions was determined by the group at the end of each session by discussing how long it would take to do the assignment. When agreement was reached, the next session was scheduled accordingly.

Each assignment was done by the managers with the same employee. When the training program was completed, each manager had completed the following steps of the performance review program with one employee:

Jointly developing significant job segments.
Jointly developing standards of performance for one significant job segment.
Completing an appraisal form.
Having the employee complete a self-appraisal form.
Conducting an appraisal interview.
Jointly developing a performance improvement plan.

After the training program was completed, the managers were scheduled to conduct performance reviews with all employees. The management development supervisor at Carlsbad was available as a resource for anyone who needed help.

According to William Simpson, management training manager at Kemper Insurance, that company's performance review training was done on a more concentrated basis. For example, a two-day workshop was conducted with Kemper managers on how to write performance standards. Here is a brief outline of the approach, adapted with permission from *Education Exchange,* a publication of the Insurance Company Education Directors Society.

FIRST DAY

Morning
1. Welcome
2. Objectives of workshop
3. Introductions

4. Background of performance standards within Kemper Insurance
5. Principal (explains *what, who, how,* and *when*)
   Film (29 minutes)
   Quiz
   Discussion
6. Need for performance standards (explains *why*)
   Filmed case study (4 minutes)
   Discussion questions
   Other
7. Procedures and techniques (explains *how*)
   Booklet, "Guidelines"
   Handout material
   Other

Lunch

Afternoon   1. Workshop: practice in writing performance standards
   Consultation with discussion leader as needed
2. Periodic summaries by participants

SECOND DAY

Morning   1. Continuing workshops in writing performance standards
   Periodic evaluation of progress by participants
   Continued consultation with discussion leader as needed
2. Assignment changes as necessary or desirable
3. Periodic summaries by participants of progress, problems, and so on
4. Informal session with guest speaker
   Presentation
   Questions and answers

Lunch

Afternoon   1. Continuing workshops
   Include periodic evaluation, periodic summaries, assignment changes, and so on
2. Summary
3. Close

This concentrated workshop was designed to develop and sharpen skills through extensive practice and critique.

Appropriate Controls Are Established

There are two philosophies of management. One says that people will do what the manager *expects*. The other says that people will do what the manager *inspects*. The first philosophy applies in many situations, but in performance appraisals, the second seems to predominate.

Even if managers are sold on the performance review program and higher management expects them to do it, there is a good chance that the reviews will be considered a should-do instead of a must-do. In most cases, the managers have so many must-do's that many of the should-do's don't get done. And if the manager discovers that nothing serious happens if the performance reviews aren't completed on schedule, the program becomes "voluntary" even though it began as a compulsory part of the job.

At one plant of a large company, the general manager was most enthusiastic when the new performance review program started. He conducted reviews with his employees as scheduled, and he expected them to do the same. The human resources department sent him a monthly report of schedules and completions. If any reviews were not completed on time, he talked with the manager about it. So all reviews were completed, most of them on time.

During the second year of the program, the general manager didn't complete his reviews as scheduled. In spite of reminders from the human resources department, he fell further and further behind. Because he hadn't completed his, he didn't say anything to his employees who hadn't completed theirs. Managers soon discovered that the program was now "voluntary." Some did it and some didn't.

During the second year, this general manager transferred to the corporate office and was replaced by a general manager from a different plant. When the new general manager learned of the performance review situation, he called the department heads together and said, "I understand you have the same performance review program here that we have at the other plant. I believe in the program. I will do it on schedule with each of my employees. I expect you to do it on schedule with your employees. I've asked the human resources manager to send me a monthly report of performance reviews scheduled and those completed. If the reviews are not completed as scheduled, I will not approve any salary increases for you or anyone else in your department until they are completed. In other words, I'm going to *require* that you do it, because I believe that it is beneficial to every employee as well as to the company. Any questions?"

Naturally, there weren't any questions. The managers knew that the program had just returned from "voluntary" to compulsory. Controls like this are sometimes needed to put performance review in the must-do category.

Summary

Performance of employees can be improved through performance appraisal and coaching. This won't happen, however, unless a program is carefully planned and effectively implemented. It won't be perfect at the beginning. Therefore, it is probably wise to start slowly, perhaps by means of a pilot program in a department where the manager is eager to try it. If the program is effective, other managers will hear about it and request that it be implemented in their departments. Eventually it may become company policy for all departments.

The five requirements described in this chapter are essential to the success of a performance review program. If any one of them is missing, there is a good chance that the program will fail. Every organization, therefore, should be sure that:

The program fits the organization.
The program is understood.
The program is sold.
The reviewers are trained.
Appropriate controls are established.

An effective performance review program can be highly beneficial, not only in terms of financial savings but also in terms of the morale of manager and employee alike.

Posttest

Write "yes" in front of each statement if you agree and "no" if you disagree.

_____ 1. Every employee has responsibility for his own development.
_____ 2. Every manager has responsibility for the growth and development of all employees.

_____ 3. Every organization has responsibility for the growth and development of all employees.

_____ 4. Most people want to know how they are doing their job as the manager sees it.

_____ 5. Most employees would like to improve their performance.

_____ 6. Less than maximum performance of an employee is often due to factors over which the employee has no control.

_____ 7. The same performance review program (forms, procedures, interview) should be used both for improved performance and for salary administration.

_____ 8. Performance appraisals and reviews should be voluntary on the part of managers.

_____ 9. The more writing required of the manager on the appraisal form, the more effective the program.

_____ 10. The less paperwork required in a performance appraisal program, the more effective the program.

_____ 11. Appraisal forms should include about a 50-50 balance between items dealing with performance and those dealing with personality.

_____ 12. Agreement on significant job segments and standards of performance is an important prerequisite to the appraisal of job performance.

_____ 13. The word "appraisal" connotes both judgment and communication.

_____ 14. A group appraisal of a person's performance is better than having an appraisal just by the manager.

_____ 15. A self-appraisal by the employee is a good idea.

_____ 16. The main objective of the appraisal interview is for the manager to explain and sell her prepared appraisal to the employee.

_____ 17. In the interview discussing the performance of the employee, there should be no surprises.

_____ 18. In an appraisal interview, it's a good idea to have at least three people present (for example, the manager, the employee, and a neutral party, such as a representative of the human resources department).

_____ 19. Appraisal interviews should be a pleasant experience for both manager and employee.

_____ 20. In the appraisal interview, the manager should not show his completed form to the employee.

_____ 21. An organization can be assured that an effective appraisal interview has been conducted if the employee is required to sign the form.

_____ 22. In an appraisal interview, the manager should always give her appraisal of the employee and then ask the employee for reactions and comments.

_____ 23. It's a good idea to divide the appraisal interview into two or three separate interviews.

_____ 24. An appraisal interview should always end on a positive note.

_____ 25. A specific written performance improvement plan is an important part of a performance review program.

_____ 26. A performance improvement plan should include what should be done, by whom, and when.

_____ 27. It's a good idea for employees to work toward performance improvement in several areas at once.

_____ 28. Coaching means the same as counseling.

_____ 29. Coaching a group of employees is similar to coaching a team of athletes.

_____ 30. On-the-job coaching is necessary to be sure that the performance improvement plan is implemented.

_____ 31. Coaching on the job should include praise for good work, as well as constructive criticism and help to improve poor work.

_____ 32. Improvement in performance should be immediately rewarded by the manager.

_____ 33. Rewards should be based on performance, rather than seniority.

_____ 34. Both the manager and the employee should have a copy of all completed forms.

_____ 35. A copy of the completed appraisal forms should be put in the personnel file of the employee.

_____ 36. A standard of performance should be:

_____   a. Established for a job.

_____   b. Established for an individual.

_____   c. An "acceptable" level of performance.

_____   d. A "well done" level of performance.

_____   e. Challenging (requires stretch but can be reached).

_____   f. Unattainable (requires stretch and can't be reached).

_____   g. Agreed on between manager and employee.

_____   h. Determined solely by the manager.

_____   i. Determined solely by the employee.

_____   j. Jointly determined by manager and employee.
_____   k. Clear to manager and employee.
_____   l. Written.
_____   m. Time oriented.
_____   n. Specific (numbers, percentages, dollars, wherever possible).
_____   o. The basis for performance appraisal.
_____   p. Subject to change.
_____ 37. The same appraisal forms and procedures can be effectively used by any kind of organization.
_____ 38. The people who supervise a performance appraisal program must do more than simply oversee paperwork. They must communicate the program and sell it to those involved.
_____ 39. It takes no real training to conduct performance reviews effectively.
_____ 40. Administrative controls must be established for performance review programs.

Test Answers and Reasons for Them

1. Yes, but it must be supplemented by items 2 and 3.
2. Yes, but it must be supplemented by items 1 and 3.
3. Yes, but it must be supplemented by items 1 and 2 to show a complete picture of the responsibilities.
4. Yes, because it relieves feelings of insecurity.
5. Yes, because it can bring rewards such as self-satisfaction, promotion, and merit salary increases.
6. Yes. Other reasons for less than maximum performance include problems inherent in the manager, poor working conditions, defective equipment or materials, and personal problems the employee cannot directly control.
7. No. There is much emotion involved in discussing salary, and usually the objective of improved performance is hard to accomplish simultaneously.
8. No. Appraisals and reviews should be compulsory to be sure they are done.
9. No, not necessarily.
10. No, not necessarily. Effectiveness may have nothing to do with the amount of paperwork.
11. No. All or nearly all of the items on an appraisal form should deal directly with performance.

12. Yes, because these two factors clarify what's expected and provide a sound basis for the appraisal.
13. No, "appraisal" connotes judgment but not communication.
14. No. Although group appraisals can help avoid bias and increase objectivity, they are very time-consuming and dilute the role of the manager in the performance review process.
15. Yes, because it generates employee involvement and also helps show the manager how the employee feels about his own performance.
16. No. The main purpose is to get understanding and agreement. The best approach is to discuss the appraisal that each of them has completed.
17. Yes, because the joint development of significant job standards and standards of performance will clarify what is expected of the employee. If expectations are clear to both manager and employee, the manager's opinion will not be a surprise. Also, the day-to-day communication and coaching should keep the employee informed of how she is doing.
18. No, only the manager and the employee should be at the appraisal interview. A third party should be added only for a specific purpose, such as to help prepare a performance improvement plan.
19. Yes, both should feel good about the interview when it is over.
20. No. The manager should not hide anything from the employee, including the appraisal form.
21. No. The only thing that a signature ensures is that the person signed the form.
22. No, this is only one possible approach. Another is to have the subordinate give his self-appraisal first.
23. Yes. This is advisable because the interview must accomplish several objectives: to agree on the appraisal, to develop a performance improvement plan, and to clarify significant job segments and standards of performance for the next appraisal period.
24. Yes. This gives both manager and employee a constructive attitude toward improving the employee's performance.
25. Yes, because it helps clarify future action for both manager and subordinate.
26. Yes. It is important for the plan to be specific.
27. No. In most cases, it is best to concentrate on only one area at a time to be sure that improvement occurs. Sometimes a second area can also be worked on.

28. No. Coaching is always job oriented and is initiated by the manager. Emphasis is placed on telling. Counseling is usually initiated by the employee and may deal with personal rather than job-related problems. Emphasis is on listening by the manager.
29. Yes. In both situations, the "coach" is trying to get maximum individual as well as team performance.
30. Yes. After the performance improvement plan is jointly developed by manager and employee, on-the-job coaching both reminds and helps the employee to implement the plan.
31. Yes, coaches should praise good work as well as correct poor work.
32. Yes. Immediate positive reinforcement by praise or other means is the best way to encourage and stimulate continued improvement in performance.
33. Yes, in order to encourage maximum effort and the best possible performance.
34. Yes. Each should have a copy for regular referral to ensure understanding and good working relationships.
35. Yes, these forms should be used in considerations for salary increases, promotions, and other personnel decisions.
36. Items a, c, g, j, k, l, m, n. o, and p should be marked "yes."
37. No, forms and procedures must fit the requirements of the specific organization. Some organizations are better equipped to handle detailed paperwork than others, for example.
38. Yes. No matter how good a program looks on paper, the people who use it must understand it and believe in it before it can really work.
39. No, training is very important. Conducting performance reviews requires skills that must be learned.
40. Yes. Unless higher management establishes requirements and controls, managers will tend to regard it as a should-do rather than a must-do.

Leaders Who Coach Create Coaching Cultures

DIANNA ANDERSON, MCC, AND MERRILL ANDERSON, Ph.D., LLC

Tom gave his coach a quizzical look, not quite sure how to take her comments. Ellen, his coach, was describing to Tom her recommendations for focusing their coaching work together. On the basis of the background information that Ellen had gathered, she could clearly see that Tom would benefit from integrating a coaching approach into his management style. Tom wasn't exactly sure what that meant, but he was certain that he didn't have time for this.

Tom prided himself on being someone who was working his way up the ladder in this manufacturing company. Tom had begun his ca-

Dianna Anderson, MCC, is vice president of leadership coaching at MetrixGlobal, LLC. She has more than fifteen years' experience as a professional coach and management consultant creating transformational change for individuals and organizations. She is the coauthor of Coaching That Counts: Harnessing the Power of Leadership Coaching to Deliver Strategic Value. She is a Master Certified Coach through the International Coach Federation. She can be reached at dianna@metrixglobal.net.
Merrill C. Anderson, Ph.D., is a business consulting executive, author, and educator with twenty years' experience improving the performance of people and organizations. Dr. Anderson is currently the chief executive officer of MetrixGlobal LLC, a professional services firm that partners with business leaders to maximize the value of people and change initiatives. He has consulted with more than 100 companies throughout the world to effectively manage strategic organization change. Dr. Anderson has more than seventy professional publications and speeches to his credit, including Coaching That Counts: Harnessing the Power of Leadership Coaching to Deliver Strategic Value and Bottom-Line Organization Development. He may be reached at merrilland@metrixglobal.net.

reer as a shop floor supervisor, and, on the strength of his many suc-
cesses, he rose to accept management responsibilities on the plant
leadership team. He was considered a high-potential leader who might
some day assume even greater leadership responsibilities for the company. Tom was well regarded by people at all levels in the plant and
maintained good working relationships. Lately, he had been losing his
cool in management meetings, which concerned the plant manger and
the HR director. It was suggested that Tom work with a coach to help
him get back on a more even keel.

Tom's coach, Ellen, had conducted interviews with Tom's direct reports, his peers on the leadership team, and his manager in order to
gain a fuller picture of Tom's strengths and his development opportunities. She learned that Tom had a strong reputation for getting things
done in the plant, often by taking the reins and personally doing whatever needed to be done. Tom's classic pace-setting style had served
him well as an individual contributor; however, he no longer had the
bandwidth to step in for all seven people who reported to him. He was
spreading himself too thin by personally taking on whatever crises
erupted. Tom was becoming exhausted, which showed up as fits of im-
patience and sometimes explosions of anger toward his peers and his
employees. He knew that something needed to change, but the idea of
coaching his people had not really occurred to him. His approach to
leadership had always been to lead by example and do whatever
needed to be done. A shift to a coaching approach would be a big
change for Tom.

The Benefits of Integrating Coaching for Leaders

At this point Tom was open to trying anything that could deliver results;
he asked Ellen to tell him more about integrating a coaching approach
into his management style. Ellen understood Tom's concern regarding
how much time it would take to learn this new approach. Tom's plate
was already filled to overflowing; there was no room to put more on
unless something came off. Ellen assured Tom that one of the first
areas of focus for their coaching would be getting Tom's personal management under control. Ellen explained that shifting to a coaching style
of management would require some investment of learning and practice time up front, but she assured Tom that it was an investment that
would pay big dividends. Ellen explained that these are some of the
benefits that Tom could expect if he starts coaching his staff:

1. *People will start to find their own answers.* Tom had become what Ellen described as an "answer-dispensing machine." Tom's staff sought him out frequently to ask him questions of all kinds. Pressed for time, Tom had fallen into the habit of dispensing answers, just like a vending machine—insert a question, get an answer. As a result, Tom spent a lot of his day answering questions. Ellen pointed out that if Tom starts to coach his employees instead, by asking them questions to solicit their own insights about situations, his employees will begin to find their own answers. Eventually, Ellen assured Tom, they will gain enough confidence in their own abilities that they will take action without having to ask Tom what to do. There was a certain logic to this that appealed to Tom. And he was drawn to the possibility of getting out of the answer-vending business.

2. *People will become more resourceful.* Consistent developmental coaching brings out the best in people. Ellen pointed out that as an outcome of receiving coaching, Tom's staff will begin to see new possibilities. With each new skill they try out, or problem that they solve, they will discover that they have more gifts and abilities than they are aware of. The learning that coaching stimulates becomes reinforcing, and leaders who are coached often continue to cultivate their own learning even when they are not directly being coached. In this way the benefits of coaching cascade throughout the organization.

3. *People will start to integrate a coaching approach into their behavior.* Coaching is contagious. Ellen told Tom that it is likely that his staff will begin to emulate his coaching style, becoming less directive with their own staffs.

4. *The manager will have more time and space for the strategic part of his job.* Ellen explained that as Tom's employees become more independent, they will be able to take on more responsibility with less day-to-day supervision. As a result, she noted, he will have more time and space to focus on the strategic initiatives that he is feeling so guilty about neglecting.

5. *The manager will be able to work more effectively with his peers and others.* Tom had a reputation for coming up with innovative ideas for improving performance at the plant. The challenge that he consistently faced was getting the leadership team to get behind the ideas that he presented. Regardless of how logical his arguments were, he often could not get certain members of the team to buy in. Ellen pointed out that he could use some of the coaching skills that he would learn to engage his colleagues in dialogues about the underlying causes of their

resistance. Once the core of the resistance is understood, meaningful actions can be taken to move through the challenges.

This all sounded good to Tom, and he told Ellen that he was looking forward to getting started with coaching.

Evoking the Coach Within

At first, Tom's coaching was focused on his personal development. Ellen helped Tom to see that the adrenaline high he was riding most days was contributing to his feelings of being overwhelmed. Through coaching, Tom learned to set more reasonable boundaries around his work, manage his schedule to give himself some time to focus on what was most important, and find his center when he felt himself heading toward a blow-up. With practice and patience, Tom soon found himself feeling more at ease. With his own life feeling less frenetic, Tom now had the presence and perspective he needed to begin to integrate coaching into his management style.

Ellen guided Tom to find opportunities to stop telling people what to do and start helping them to discover a path forward for themselves. Tom learned how to listen to people on multiple levels. He started to tune into how they were feeling, what they valued, and even what they were not saying. He started to ask questions that opened up their thinking and helped them to see situations from different perspectives. Most important, he stopped trying to solve every problem himself and began taking great pride in how his staff was taking charge of challenges that it had previously shied away from.

The transition to a coaching approach had felt awkward at first. And although it did initially take more time to offer coaching that it did to dispense answers, Tom felt that it well worth the effort.

Tom soon found that coaching was becoming a natural part of his life. He used a coaching approach to offer feedback to others, to handle difficult conversations, and to share his ideas. Tom was delighted to discover that by tuning into the emotional context of situations and responding to underlying dynamics, he was able to find creative solutions to problems that had been roadblocks in the past. As his coaching confidence increased, Tom was ready to expand his coaching approach beyond improving the performance of his staff and to take a coaching approach to creating organizational change.

Tom's plant faced intense pressure to reduce costs, driven mainly by the rising cost of steel, in the manufacturing process. Tom believed that by applying lean manufacturing principals, the plant could make significant process improvements. Since Tom supervised only one section of the plant, he would have to work with the leadership team to move this project forward. He used his coaching time with Ellen to think through a plan of action and to role-play some of the more challenging conversations and presentations that he would need to conduct in order to gain buy-in from everyone involved.

As he moved forward with the project, he found that taking a coaching approach was invaluable. It was not that he was coaching everyone, but he was using the coaching approach of evoking the insight of the people he worked with in order to bring the collective insight and knowledge of the plant to bear against this important challenge. As is typical with change projects, some people became inspired by the opportunity to try new approaches, while others hung back, uncertain of the change. Overall, the project was a huge success and resulted in a 30 percent reduction in defectives and a dramatic reduction in no-shows for the line workers.

As the coaching relationship between Ellen and Tom was drawing to a close, Ellen reflected back to Tom the transformation that he had gone through. He had started out as a pace-setting manager who dispensed answers on demand and felt perpetually overwhelmed and had emerged as an inspiring leader who evoked insight from others and was leading a complex change effort. He was happier, he felt more successful, and he was very proud of how he was supporting his colleagues to make meaningful change. Moreover, his entire department was operating more smoothly as it embraced a coaching approach. With Tom's guidance, the leadership team had come together around the process improvement project, and change was under way in the plant.

The Elements of a Coaching Approach

The preceding case study illuminates the extensive impact that a coaching approach can have on an organization. The latest return-on-investment (ROI) studies on leadership coaching reveal ROI in the range of 500 to 700 percent. With these kinds of results, it's little wonder that organizations are eager to create a culture of coaching in which all employees learn how to integrate coaching skills into their approach to work.

Before we start to look at instilling a coaching approach on a larger scale, let's first take a look at the elements of Tom's development. We need to grasp the underlying dynamics that made his transformation so successful in order to be able to replicate them with larger groups. The three essential elements for integrating coaching into Tom's management style were:

1. Training in coaching skills
2. The experience of being coached
3. The development of personal insight

Let's take a look at Tom's experience to understand how these elements work together to transform his leadership style.

1. *Training in Coaching Skills*. Tom received personalized training in coaching skills through his work with Ellen. Ellen introduced coaching concepts as they were appropriate to the issues that Tom brought to the coaching sessions. Ellen naturally started with the fundamental skills of listening and questioning. As Tom gained confidence with the basics, Ellen introduced more complex coaching approaches.

2. *The Experience of Being Coached*. To fully appreciate the power of coaching to release untapped potential, managers need to have the experience of being coached by a competent coach. It was not until Tom experienced the "aha" of seeing something from a totally new perspective, or understanding how he was unwittingly contributing to a problem, that he truly appreciated the transformational power of coaching. *Real* coaching is not an intellectual process; it is a visceral experience that resonates deeply on many levels. Without this "aha" experience, coaching remains very superficial.

3. *The Development of Personal Insight.* The key enabler for people to move beyond superficial issues and to access deeper levels is *insight*. Research presented in our book *Coaching That Counts*[1] was drawn from several evaluations of executive coaching initiatives. This research indicated that deepening the levels of insight of the leaders being coached was the driving force behind how these leaders created value for themselves and for the organization. As leaders progressed through their coaching relationships, they were able to tap into deeper levels of insight, which in turn allowed them to have greater impact on the organization in which they worked. Four levels of insight were identified: reflective, emotional, intuitive, and inspirational.

You can see this dynamic of deepening insight at work as Tom progressed through coaching. Initially, the focus of his coaching work was on his personal development, where he reflected upon patterns of behavior (the first level of insight, reflective) and noted how his actions contributed to his feels of being overwhelmed. As Tom became more centered, he began to focus his coaching on interpersonal relation-ships, such as coaching his direct reports. In these coaching interac-tions, Tom began to use his emotions as a barometer to guide his coaching approach (the second level of insight is emotional). He found that by tuning into the emotional context of situations, he could dis-cern how best to move the action forward. These experiences gave Tom the confidence to tackle the issue of reducing production costs for the plant and gave him the skills he needed to work through more complex issues. As he moved into this new space, Tom relied on his intuitive understanding of what was possible, coupled with his linear analytic capability, to chart a path forward (third level of insight, intuitive). As Tom continues to grow as a manager, it is possible that he will progress to the fourth level of insight, where he will be inspired to take original actions to transform himself and his organization in significant ways.

The development of insight is essential for coaching to have strate-gic impact; without insight, coaching remains tactical. Tactical coach-ing tends to work with surface-level issues, such as getting more organized and resolving minor disagreements. While valuable, this type of coaching definitely represents the shallow end of the coaching pool. Transformational coaching is development that occurs on a number of levels and is aimed at transforming the individuals who receive coach-ing and the organizations in which they work. If Tom's coaching work had concluded when he stopped being an answer-dispensing manager, there would have been real value. However, the fact that he continued to deepen his learning and take on the challenge of influencing the entire plant demonstrates the impact that transformational coaching can have.

Creating a Coaching Culture

The generally accepted approach for creating a coaching culture is to train the managers in coaching skills. This typically takes the form of having all managers (and sometimes all employees) take part in a one- to two-day coaching-skills training program. While this "sheep-dipping" approach can be helpful for introducing the concepts of coaching, it rarely, if ever, by itself results in the integration of a coach-ing philosophy into the fabric of the organization. If the intention of creating a culture of coaching is to transform an organization into an environment where the potential that is resident in the organization is cultivated and translated into strategic outcomes, then the culture that is created needs to rest firmly on the dynamics of transformational coaching.

Returning to our case study, let's look at how the underlying elements of Tom's development can be applied to larger settings. While it would be ideal to replicate Tom's experience with every manager in the organization and to provide all managers with their own leadership coach to personally guide them through the coaching process, this approach is clearly impractical from a monetary and logistical perspective. What is needed is an alternative approach that inculcates coaching into the organizational culture in a more practical and affordable way.

As business leaders and human resource professionals face the challenge of creating coaching cultures in their organizations, we suggest that they keep the following guidelines in mind:

1. *Set a clear strategic intent for the move to a coaching culture.* Any kind of shift in culture takes patience, commitment, and a clear intention on the part of the leadership of the organization to make the change happen. Without a clear and compelling story that outlines the benefit to the organization for making the change, culture change initiatives can have a tendency to wither on the vine. Also, in order for the change to stick, a case must also be made for how individual leaders and employees will also benefit.

2. *Provide a foundation for coaching as an essential developmental process.* Make sure that leadership competency models appropriately feature coaching as an essential set of knowledge, skills, and abilities. Ensure that demonstrating successful coaching factors into succession planning decisions. Align educational curricula to support the development of the coaching capabilities of leaders along the lines of the tiered approach discussed in item 3.

3. *Select the highest-potential leaders to develop coaching capabilities.* Many organizations have a select group of high-potential leaders. These leaders are expected to assume greater responsibilities and more quickly be promoted into senior roles. The development of coaching capabilities can accelerate the readiness of these leaders. It is clear that by integrating a coaching approach into his management style, Tom was able to improve his ability to collaborate with peers on the lean-manufacturing initiative. Consequently, he demonstrated greater readiness to take on additional challenges and more responsibility. When the intention is to create a coaching culture, then the selection of leaders to develop coaching capabilities becomes even more important. Se-

lect the highest-potential, most influential leaders to participate in coaching development. These "seeds" then spread a coaching approach into their organizations by example and influence the cascading of coaching into their respective organizations.

4. *Adopt a tiered approach to learning.* Rather than sheep-dipping, where everyone has the same experience, customize the training to the particular needs of groups of people. One of the ways that organizations have successfully made Six-Sigma quality initiatives part of their culture is by offering varying levels of Six-Sigma training to people in the organization. Not everyone needs to have the same level of training. So, for example, people who need only a basic level understanding of Six Sigma become "yellow belts" by receiving a one-day session. "Green belts," or those people who will work part-time on a Six-Sigma project, receive one week of training. "Black belts" receive a month's worth of training because they will work full-time on Six-Sigma-quality initiatives.

A similar tiered approach to training people to integrate coaching into their management style can be adopted. Those people who require only a passing knowledge of coaching, for example, key leaders who manage technology rather than people, might receive a half-day overview of coaching. At the other end of the range, key leaders of departments or divisions that will be expected to emerge as role models for coaching might receive more extensive training and coaching experience. This tiered approach focuses the investment in coach training resources where it will realize the greatest return.

5. *Integrate personal development into the coach training curricula.* Coaching that delivers transformational change taps into deep levels of insight for both the coach and the coachee. Therefore, it is essential that leaders who are cultivating coaching capabilities also develop their personal insight as part of that training process. Without the development of insight, coaching remains a tactic that just skims the surface, rather than getting to the heart of the matter.

6. *Measure results.* A comprehensive evaluation strategy to track and measure the impact of coaching development initiatives allows an organization to understand how a coaching development program is adding value and provides those who are managing the initiative with the information required to make midcourse corrections. The regular reporting of metrics sends a clear message to people in the organization that coaching is about the creation of value for the business and not just an exercise for the participants. These metrics should reflect

the strategic intentions for coaching and provide feedback on how successfully the coaching culture is being realized. For example, assessments may reveal that leaders are building their competencies in coaching. Or trend lines may indicate that a number of leaders who experienced coaching are "ready now" to take on additional responsibilities.

Conclusion

Coaching is more than a set of skills; it is a rich, holistic approach for releasing the potential in people and in organizations. Tom's experience demonstrates that managers with very different management styles, such as pace-setting and directive, can learn to integrate coaching into their management style if they are provided with the right mix of coaching support and personal development.

The creation of a coaching culture in an organization does not happen overnight. In fact, it is likely to take years to accomplish. Any journey, the saying goes, begins with the first step. With coaching, the first step is selecting those leaders who are highly regarded and influential to participate in the coaching-development process. This sends a strong signal to others about the importance of coaching in the organization. Coaching needs to be supported in the organization by integrating coaching into the mix of leadership competencies and by making coaching a part of the process of selecting, developing, and promoting leaders. Coaching cascades in the organization when the right ingredients are present: the strategic intent for coaching is communicated, leaders embrace coaching as a required competency, and training and development activities are made available to people. It becomes a strategic initiative when a critical mass of leaders is participating in the coaching development process.

The creation of a coaching culture is an investment, and, like any investment, it should be made with thoughtful consideration of how to realize the greatest returns for the organization. The returns can be considerable, for, as leaders are transformed through the experience of coaching and being coached, they transform the organizations in which they work.

Note

1. D. L. Anderson and M. C. Anderson, *Coaching That Counts: Harnessing the Power of Leadership Coaching to Deliver Strategic Value* (Burlington, Mass.: Elsevier Butterworth–Heinemann, 2005).

CHAPTER 8

Evaluating a Training Course on Performance Appraisal and Coaching

This case study shows what a company can do if it wants to upgrade its performance appraisal process. In my experience, the human resources managers and line managers I have talked with are not happy with their programs. There seems to be a constant revision of philosophy, objectives, forms, and procedures. Most organizations are still using performance appraisal to decide on salary adjustments and provide information for personnel decisions including promotion and termination. This book concentrates on programs designed to *improve performance*. If you are looking for training to help you improve your program, this case study will be of great interest. You can see what Kemper did and its results. The evaluation process was based on the Kirkpatrick "four-level" model for determining the effectiveness of the training.

Kemper National Insurance Companies

Judith P. Clarke, Training Manager
Corporate Education Department, Long Grove, Illinois

This chapter is based on Donald L. Kirkpatrick, *Evaluating Training Programs: The Four Levels*, 2nd ed. (San Francisco: Berrett-Koehler, 1998).

Need and Purpose

Our training program is a success if it accomplishes four objectives: participants like the program, participants gain needed knowledge and skills, participants apply what they learned to their jobs, and participants assist the company in achieving its mission and objectives. The purpose of the program is to improve performance. The purpose of evaluation is to verify and improve the effectiveness of training. The evaluation design includes ways and means of measuring the effectiveness of the program in achieving each of the four objectives just defined.

The Training Course

The program was conducted at the Charlotte branch of Kemper. All supervisors and managers attended the course during a three-month period between December 1989 and March 1990. The program and its evaluation received the complete support of the branch manager. Figure 8-1 describes the program content and objectives.

Evaluation Design

Both quantitative and qualitative data were collected. Data collection techniques included existing tools as well as measurements designed for this evaluation. This section describes the data collection tools that we used for the four levels on which we evaluated the training program.

1. *Reaction.* How well did the participants like the training? Each participant completed the reaction sheet shown in Figure 8-2 at the end of the course. The results were tabulated and summarized.

2. *Learning.* What knowledge and skills did participants gain from the program? We collected data by administering the Performance Appraisal Skills Inventory (the Organization Design and Development, available from King of Prussia, Penn.) before and after training. The inventory contains eighteen performance appraisal situations. For each situation, the participant selects the best answer from four possible choices.

3. *Behavior.* To what extent have participants transferred knowledge and skills learned in the program to their jobs in these four areas: preparing for the performance appraisal, establishing two-way communication with employees, gaining agreement on the appraisal, and documenting the report form?

To collect data, we used results from the performance appraisal report form checklist shown in Figure 8-3, administered before and

(text continues on page 134)

Figure 8-1. Performance appraisal and coaching seminar.

Objectives

During this course, participants will:

1. Self-assess individual strengths and weaknesses in the skill areas necessary to establish two-way communication and gain agreement in the six steps of the performance appraisal discussion:

- Building trust
- Opening
- Accomplishments and concerns
- Planning
- Evaluating and rating
- Closing

2. Identify individual improvement goals for strengthening skills needed for conducting effective performance appraisal discussions.

3. Practice applying the following coaching process to the six steps of the performance appraisal discussion:

- Identify the situation.
- Clarify information.
- Explore options.
- Agree on actions.
- Follow up.

4. Learn to recognize when specific coaching techniques can be used to establish two-way communication and reduce defensiveness during the performance appraisal discussion.

5. Analyze various ways in which both the employee and the supervisor can prepare for the performance appraisal discussion:

- Reviewing objectives, standards, and reports
- Employee self-appraisal
- Input from next-level manager

6. Define each section of the performance appraisal report form and explain how to use it as a tool in the performance appraisal discussion.

7. Explain how the wording of the performance appraisal report form can enhance the clarity of the completed form and reinforce the interactive tone of the overall process.

8. Demonstrate ability in writing

- Performance improvement needs
- Performance improvement objectives
- Achievement of prior objectives

9. Identify the criteria for a timely, high-quality performance appraisal report form through the use of a checklist.

Figure 8-2. Reaction sheet.

Course Title: _____

Instructor(s): _____   Date: _____

Your evaluation of this course will assist in making future courses more effective.

A. *Instructions:* Please indicate a rating for each statement below by circling a number on the scale to the right:

	Strongly agree				*Strongly disagree*

1. Course objectives were clearly stated and easily understood.
    Comments: 5   4   3   2   1

2. Course objectives were met.
    Comments: 5   4   3   2   1

3. Course met my personal expectations.
    Comments: 5   4   3   2   1

4. Time allotted for various segments was appropriate.   5   4   3   2   1
    Comments:

	High				*Low*

5. To what degree was the course relevant to your job?   5   4   3   2   1
    Comments:

6. How would you rate your personal interest in this course?   5   4   3   2   1
    Comments:

B. To what degree did the following contribute to your achieving the course objectives?

7. Printed participant materials (e.g., participant guide, handouts).   5   4   3   2   1
    Comments:

8. Audiovisual materials (e.g., tapes, videos, overheads)   5   4   3   2   1
    Comments:

9. Discussion(s) with other participants.   5   4   3   2   1
    Comments:

Figure 8-3. Performance appraisal report form checklist.

On the basis of the completed appraisals that you have brought to the course, how would you answer these questions?

	Yes	No
Performance Standards		
• Do standards reflect the current job?	☐	☐
• Are standards attached and evaluated?	☐	☐
Attendance		
• Are attendance problems documented according to policy?	☐	☐
• Have you refrained from describing the personal reasons for absences?	☐	☐
Achievement of Prior Objectives		
• Are prior objectives restated and evaluated?	☐	☐
• If prior objectives are not met, are clear circumstances or reasons stated?	☐	☐
• If prior objectives are not met, will an outside reader know how this will affect the performance rating?	☐	☐
Attributes		
• Are attributes coded properly and supported by job-specific behavioral examples?	☐	☐
• Are attributes used to recognize and reinforce past performance?	☐	☐
Performance Improvement Needs: Immediate Needs		
• Do the needs relate to failure to meet standards or achieve objectives?	☐	☐
• Do supporting comments indicate a sense of urgency about the need?	☐	☐
• Are supporting comments job related and specific?	☐	☐
• Do supporting comments reflect input that the employee provided about the need?	☐	☐
Performance Improvement Needs: Other		
• Are the needs specific, and do they involve job-related areas that require improvement?	☐	☐
• Are they related to the current position?	☐	☐
• Do supporting comments reflect input that the employee provided about the need?	☐	☐
Objectives		
• Are performance improvement objectives listed first and linked to the need in the preceding sections?	☐	☐
• Do they state specifically how well the employee should do or achieve?	☐	☐
• Do they state specifically what the employee should do or achieve to be acceptable?	☐	☐
• Do they state specifically under what conditions (time frame, resources, training) the employee should perform?	☐	☐
• Do supporting comments reflect input that the employee provided about the objectives?	☐	☐

Performance Rating

- Is the rating consistent with the results and narrative of the entire performance analysis? ☐ ☐
- Is the rating based on the principle of zero-based appraisal? ☐ ☐

Development Objectives (if applicable)

- Is it clear that development objectives are not used in determining the performance indicator? ☐ ☐
- Is it clear that they are not requirements or standards of the current job? ☐ ☐
- Are these objectives specific in terms of what the employee should do, how well, and under what conditions? ☐ ☐
- Do supporting comments reflect input that the employee provided about the objective? ☐ ☐

Promotability

- Do identified position(s) fit the employee's experience and skills? ☐ ☐
- Are listed position(s) properly titled and coded? ☐ ☐
- If the employee is immediately promotable to another functional area, has the performance appraisal been signed by another department manager? ☐ ☐

Relocation

- Did you discuss current relocation preferences with the employee at the time of the appraisal? ☐ ☐

Supervisor's Comments

- Are the comments job related and consistent with the rest of the appraisal? ☐ ☐
- Does the Comments section effectively summarize the appraisal? ☐ ☐

Other

- Have you completed each section with all the required documentation? ☐ ☐
- If the employee is participating in the career development program, is the career development plan properly completed and attached? ☐ ☐
- Does the appraisal reflect evidence of two-way communication? ☐ ☐
- Does the appraisal language reflect employee input? ☐ ☐
- If a third party reviewed the completed appraisal, would the documentation be clear and consistent throughout each section? ☐ ☐
- Is the appraisal free of references to personal issues and circumstances of employee's life? ☐ ☐
- Has the appraisal been completed by the due date? ☐ ☐

after training; the performance appraisal questionnaire for managers, shown in Figure 8-4; the performance appraisal questionnaire for employees, shown in Figure 8-5; and unobtrusive data, which included informal observations obtained from many sources, including the human resources manager, the immediate supervisor of those completing forms and conducting interviews, and those who completed forms and conducted interviews.

4. *Results.* To assess the results, we asked this question: What gain has there been in the achievement of the following two human resources objectives? Ninety-five percent of all performance appraisals are completed on schedule, and the quality and accuracy of the appraisals improve in five areas: candidness, completeness, developmental plans, ratings, and feedback.

Data were collected through an analysis by the branch human resources manager of completed performance appraisals.

Evaluation Results

The evaluations were conducted as planned, and the results were communicated to executives and other interested and concerned persons as follows.

The performance appraisal and coaching course was designed to improve the skills of managers and supervisors in coaching effectively during the performance appraisal discussion and in writing the performance appraisal report.

The Charlotte branch was selected as the site for piloting the course and for evaluating its effectiveness. The training received the enthusiastic support of the branch manager, Jim Murphy, and of the branch human resources manager, Peggy Jones, and it was positively received by the Charlotte supervisors and managers. Forty-one branch supervisors and managers completed the course between December and March, a fact that made it possible to study the effectiveness of training with an entire management staff.

Procedure and Findings

Evaluation that verifies and improves the effectiveness of training is conducted at four levels: reaction, learning, behavior, and results. Evidence to determine the effectiveness of training must be gathered at each level. Table 8-1 lists the questions that need to be answered at each

Figure 8-4. Performance appraisal questionnaire for managers.

Instructions: This survey is designed to describe your experiences in conducting performance appraisals since completing the performance appraisal and coaching course.

Please answer the questions below by circling the number that corresponds to your response.

1. Characterize your preparation for conducting performance appraisals since completing the course.

	Much easier		Same		More difficult
Preparation is	5	4	3	2	1

Comments:

2. Characterize the actual performance appraisal discussions that you have conducted since completing the course.

	Much easier		Same		More difficult
• Discussing employee strengths	5	4	3	2	1
• Discussing performance problems	5	4	3	2	1
• Overcoming defensiveness	5	4	3	2	1
• Developing an improvement plan	5	4	3	2	1

3. Characterize your documentation of the performance appraisal report form since completing the course.

	Much easier		Same		More difficult
• Documenting performance improvement needs	5	4	3	2	1
• Writing objectives	5	4	3	2	1
• Documenting achievement of prior objectives	5	4	3	2	1

4. To what degree have you been successful in reaching agreement with your employees on the main issues of the performance appraisal discussion since completing the course?

	High		Medium		Low
	5	4	3	2	1

Comments:

5. Which aspects of the performance appraisal process are still the most difficult for you? Check your response(s):

_____ Preparing for the performance appraisal

_____ Discussing employee strengths

_____ Discussing performance problems

_____ Developing an improvement plan

(continues)

Figure 8-4. Continued.

_____ Overcoming defensiveness
_____ Conducting the performance appraisal discussion
_____ Reaching agreement on main issues
_____ Documenting performance improvement needs
_____ Writing objectives
_____ Documenting achievement of prior objectives

Please comment on the items that you have checked.

What other comments would you like to make on conducting performance appraisals? (Use the back of this sheet if necessary.)

Please use the enclosed envelope to return the completed questionnaire. Thank you for your cooperation.

level of evaluation and the data collection tools that were used in answering each question.

The findings at each level of evaluation indicate that the performance appraisal and coaching course makes a difference in increasing both the quality of the coaching that takes place during the discussion and the quality of the performance appraisal report.

Reaction. Level 1 findings indicate that course participants were satisfied customers. The course evaluations received confirmed that participants reacted positively to the course. Positive reactions increase participants' receptivity to the knowledge and skills presented in the course. The majority of participants felt that the course objectives had been met and that the course was highly relevant to their jobs. The average overall rating on a 5-point scale was 4.37.

Learning. Level 2 findings indicate that course participants made gains in the knowledge and skills needed to conduct and document quality performance appraisals. Data gathered from administration of the quality checklist before and after training indicate that 94 percent of the performance appraisals written by participants after the course were of higher quality than the appraisals that they had written before training. It was also significant that, while appraisal quality was as low as 54

Figure 8-5. Performance appraisal questionnaire for employees.

Instructions: Your manager recently completed a course on performance appraisal. In order to better understand the effectiveness of this course, we are interested in your reactions to your most recent performance appraisal.

Since this questionnaire is anonymous, do *not* sign your name.

Please answer the questions below by circling your response or the number that corresponds to your response.

1. Has your most recent performance appraisal occurred within the last six months?   Yes   No

2. Were you asked to prepare for the performance appraisal discussion?   Yes   No

   If yes, explain what you did to prepare.

3. During the performance appraisal discussion, what percentage of time did you spend talking?   ____%

   Comments:

4. Overall, how would you rate your degree of involvement in your most recent performance appraisal discussion?

High		*Medium*		*Low*
5	4	3	2	1

   Comments:

5. To what degree did your manager listen to your input during the performance appraisal discussion?

High		*Medium*		*Low*
5	4	3	2	1

   Comments:

6. To what degree did your manager consider your ideas to be important during the performance appraisal discussion?

High		*Medium*		*Low*
5	4	3	2	1

   Comments:

7. To what degree were you and your manager successful in reaching agreement on the main issues of the performance appraisal discussion?

High		*Medium*		*Low*
5	4	3	2	1

   Comments:

Please use the enclosed envelope to return the completed questionnaire. Thank you for your cooperation.

Table 8-1. Evaluation questions and data collection tools.

	Evaluation Question	*Data Collection Tool*
Reaction	How did the participants react to the training?	Course reaction sheets
Learning	What information and skills were gained?	Performance appraisal checklist administered before and after training
Behavior	How have participants transferred knowledge and skills to their jobs?	Performance appraisal checklist administered before and after training Manager and employee questionnaires Anecdotal data
Results	What effect has training had on the organization and achievement of its objectives? (Timeliness and quality in performance appraisals are a corporate goal.)	Performance appraisal checklist.

percent before training, the lowest quality observed after training was 78 percent.

Behavior. Level 3 findings provide evidence that course participants applied the knowledge and skills acquired in the course when they conducted subsequent performance appraisals. Data gathered with the quality checklist before and after training highlighted three areas of particular improvement: two-way discussion, documentation of attributes, and objectives. The course provides practice sessions to enhance skills needed to involve employees in the performance appraisal discussion and to show evidence of discussion and employee input in the performance appraisal report. Appraisals conducted after participation in the course showed nearly four times more two-way discussion after the course than before it.

Performance appraisals are audited by branch human resources staff to identify errors and potential problems. When errors are found, a performance appraisal is returned to the appraising supervisor for improvement. Strong evidence that participants applied knowledge and skills learned in the course on the job was provided by an immediate decline in the number of returns. Before the training program, eight appraisals were returned for improvement in one month. After the program, no more than two appraisals per month were returned.

The Charlotte branch human resources manager reported that,

from the conclusion of the study through the fourth quarter, the number of appraisals returned through the audit had remained low in comparison to previous years. Her report shows the percentage of audited appraisals that were of acceptable quality each quarter after the program:

Q3	90%
Q4	96
Q1	95
Q2	80
Q3	95
Q4	96

The lower quality of appraisals during the second quarter of the second year reflects the fact that five appraisals were returned for clarification of objectives and documentation of the achievement of prior objectives and that one appraisal lacked proper documentation of attendance. The Charlotte branch human resources manager is continuing to coach the management staff in these areas, but she states that the narratives now indicate much more two-way discussion than she saw before the training took place.

Another indication that participants applied new knowledge and skills was the results of two questionnaires. One questionnaire was designed for management staff who were trained and the other for the employees who reported to them.

The manager questionnaire showed that 77 percent of the management staff considered handling performance problems within the performance appraisal to be easier after taking the course. Because the skills needed to coach employees with performance improvement needs effectively are practiced during the course, supervisors and managers are likely to find handling performance problems easier because they are more skilled at doing so.

The employee questionnaire was designed to determine how the employees who had been appraised by the trained supervisors felt about how they had been coached. Evidence provided by employees indicated that supervisors were effective in three important areas: employees felt that supervisors listened (83 percent), that supervisors valued their input highly (75 percent), and that agreement was reached on main issues of the performance appraisal (77 percent).

Anecdotal data provided by the human resources manager and the participants themselves confirmed that the course had made a difference in the quality of the performance appraisals being written. By the end of the first quarter after the program, the human resources manager stated that she was seeing a marked difference in the overall quality of performance appraisals. Participants commented that it was much easier to do the appraisal after they had completed the course.

Results. Level 4 findings were drawn from data collected with the quality checklist before and after training. The course increased the quality of performance appraisals in several important areas: objectives, performance feedback, and completeness. Specific objectives that met the quality criteria presented in the course increased by 36 percent after training.

Performance feedback, both in recognizing employee strengths and in coaching for performance improvement, was of higher quality after the course. The number of appraisals containing attributes supported by behavioral examples of how the employee exhibited the attribute on the job increased by 49 percent.

Additional evidence of effective feedback on performance improvement needs was provided by the 36 percent increase found in specific objectives, which clearly state what the employee will do to maintain or improve performance and how measurement will take place. The language used to document objectives indicates that employees are becoming more involved in discussing and finding solutions to performance issues. Data from the checklist after training showed a 35 percent increase in evidence of discussion.

Conclusions and Recommendations

The evidence presented in this report supports the assumption that the performance appraisal and coaching course results in supervisors and managers who are more confident and competent in conducting quality performance appraisals. The evidence also shows an increase in the number of performance appraisal reports documented correctly.

Skills and knowledge gained during training need to be reinforced on the job. Reinforcement is achieved when all staff are trained with support from top management. Managers who have themselves been trained can coach the supervisors who report to them. Human resources staff can also provide ongoing coaching.

Training all supervisors and managers in one location creates a great opportunity for affecting the culture in terms of the overall desired outcome of the course. The evaluation clearly shows that supervisors now use a joint problem-solving approach to encourage employees to assume responsibility for their own performance. It also shows that supervisors provide candid feedback on all aspects of performance. Managers and supervisors who are more comfortable with the authoritarian management style may find this approach uncomfortable, but when it is modeled and reinforced by their own manager and peers, change is likely to occur.

CHAPTER 9

Case Study: Carilion Health System

Here is a practical case study that includes performance appraisal, the development of a performance improvement plan, and follow-up coaching to improve employee performance. It contains principles, forms, and techniques that can be adapted to any size or type of organization.

Creating Synergy Between Coaching and Performance Management

JEANNE ARMENTROUT, RN, MSN, FABC, AND CHERYL BENNETT, RN, MSN
CARILION HEALTH SYSTEM CORPORATE UNIVERSITY, ROANOKE, VIRGINIA

Performance management is a continuous process in which the manager engages in two-way communication with employees regarding

Susan H. Gebelein, Lisa A. Stevens, Carol J. Skube, David G. Lee, Brian L. Davis, and Lowell W. Hellervik, *The Successful Manager's Handbook, 6th ed.* (Minneapolis: Personnel Decisions International, 2000).

The authors extend credit and thanks to Eyde Adams, Education Consultant, Carilion Health System; Debbie Copening, Education Consultant, Carilion Health System; Becky Dooley, Education Consultant, Carilion Health System; Linda Gardner, Education Consultant, Carilion Health System; Lori Griffith, Human Resources Assistant, Carilion Health System; Kim Hall, Education Consultant, Carilion Health System; Amy Hoots-Hendrix, Employee Communications Consultant, Carilion Health System; Charlotte Hubbard, Education Consultant, Carilion Health System; and Kay Trivett, Director, Med-Surg Unit, Carilion Health System, for their contributions.

expectations, performance, areas for development, and plans for enhancing performance. For a performance management system to be successful, it must be supported by and aligned with the company's organizational goals, culture, leadership style, operating strategy, and job design.

The components of performance management that are discussed in this chapter include:

- Performance appraisal
- The performance plan
- Developmental goals and action steps
- Application—coaching process
- Tools
- Case study

Carilion Health System is the largest employer in western Virginia, with more than 9,400 employees. Carilion's eight affiliated hospitals, Level 1 Trauma Center, Cancer Center of Western Virginia, Medical Education, and more than 150 physician practices serve our community with modern health care.

In 2004, Carilion embarked on a revision of its performance management with system priorities and initiatives as described in the system scorecard (Appendix A). A specific emphasis was placed on the creation of a common language for competencies and behaviors. In addition, a scorecard metric focusing on strategic alignment and developmental goals was established.

The following is an example of Carilion's performance management system, including defined components and a case study example.

Carilion's performance management process includes an annual written review, with established coaching priorities on developmental needs and gaps identified at the annual review and during periodic checks. Managers gather data for the review and performance plan using 360° assessments. (These assessments include reviews by a superior, peer-level, and employee viewers and customers. These are chosen on the basis of frequency of interaction.) Employees receive individualized reviews and performance plans that are agreed upon with the manager. The review consists of an appraisal tool (Appendix B) that evaluates the employee on significant responsibilities and service standards. The manager summarizes the review on the basis of observations and the 360° assessments. The performance plan includes established developmental, operational, and career goals (Appendix C). As the performance plan is implemented, a defined focus is placed on closing the gap between developmental needs, business opportunities, and operational success. To close the gap, an action plan is implemented that includes definitions, timelines and application components (Appendix C). For a successful outcome, coaching occurs between the manager and the employee. Carilion defines coaching as an active process that brings about change in an individual's thoughts, attitudes, and behaviors related to agreed-upon performance expectations.

Coaching exists as a tool for managers to engage employees in real-world situations while reinforcing expected behaviors and outcomes. Managers use coaching to support change in the work environment. Coaching builds on the manager's belief that individuals are accountable for their actions and decisions and that they have the resources to solve their own challenges.

The manager-as-coach uncovers talents and resources that were not previously imagined. By showing genuine interest, the manager improves relationships and builds on talent through use of the following:

- Asking questions
- Giving clear direction
- Giving feedback
- Improving performance through a learning and growth environment
- Stimulating creativity and motivation to act

Carilion managers coach employees on a continuous basis utilizing formal and informal opportunities. Carilion's Corporate University team created a formal definition, model, and process that is utilized (Appendix D). The following case study is an example of a Carilion director coaching her newly acquired manager in a formal manner.

In a manager-as-coach scenario, the need for coaching is established during the performance review process. In this case, the director, Susan, acquired a new manager, Don, through consolidation of departments within Nursing Services.

1. *Establish the need.* Susan reviews Don's current performance plan and other available data, completes the 360° assessment process, and develops Don's annual review. Operationally, Don is not meeting his established targets for length of stay and staff turnover; in addition,

he is not scoring at meets-standard on quality measures. Developmentally, 360°s reveal negative attitude, poor communication skills, and lack of knowledge and application to develop his employees.

Susan shares the review and performance plan with Don and discusses the plan for progression, which includes coaching as an action step. The plan is agreed upon. The first phase of Don's coaching focuses on communication.

The following is Don's initial performance plan:

PERFORMANCE PLAN

Progress on current performance period goals and action plans:
Developmental goals and action plans for next performance period: growth needs to occur to obtain the goal
Developmental Goal: Department Operations—Improve turnover, length-of-stay, and quality measures through development of a solution-focused environment.
Action Steps: 1. Develop a retention plan with staff input. 2. Identify barriers to meeting length-of-service and quality targets, and develop plan for improvement. 3. Engage in a coaching relationship to improve skills.
Developmental Goal: Improve communication.
Action Steps: 1. Recognize defensive approach and nonverbal posture. 2. Identify peer mentor to give feedback after team and committee meetings regarding defensive versus offensive approaches. 3. Stop and redirect conversation when defensiveness identified.

2. *Create a relationship.* Typically, the manager-as-coach already has an established relationship with the coachee. Since this case involved a new relationship, both relationship and readiness for change developed simultaneously. The first two coaching sessions were spent uncovering expectations and Don's vision and goals for his unit.

3. *Evaluate readiness for change.* As the relationship develops, Don's readiness for change becomes apparent to Susan. At this point, Don decides if he is willing to put forth the effort to make the necessary changes. With this decision, he has the option to leave the role.

4. *Determine commitment to coaching.* Don is ready and eager to accept coaching because he has the desire to be an exceptional leader. Susan understands the time intensity on her part.

5. *Use discovery and observation.* The 360° assessment only scratches the surface with regard to Don's developmental needs. Susan

has not directly observed Don's leadership skills, so it is necessary for her to see his day-to-day activities. Susan's goal is to spend time observing Don in situations in which she can see the leadership skills that have an impact on his developmental plan.

Susan observes Don in a staff meeting, leading and interacting with his staff. Susan also spends a day on Don's unit observing his staff and then his communication skills as they impact the team. Susan inquires about Don's unit's vision and goals, and whether employees are aware of them. This helps Susan define what the specific communication issues are, ensure that the performance plan is on track, and develop more defined action steps.

6. *Establish the plan: specific action strategies.* The following are the specific strategies and revised performance plan, based on new data:

PERFORMANCE PLAN

Developmental goals and action plans for next performance period: growth needs to occur to obtain the goal
Developmental Goal: Communication—Create an environment that is positive and focused on improvement.
Action Steps: 1. Highlight success in written formats, meetings, and make them visible to your coach. 2. Focus on process improvement, and bring solutions, not just issues. 3. Choose one quality initiative to improve, and include staff. 4. Read Chapter 21 in *The Successful Manager's Handbook,*[1] 6th ed. and prepare to discuss at next one-on-one meeting.
Developmental Goal: Communication—Develop and inspire staff.
Action Steps: 1. Rewrite vision, using interpretive statements, and communicate and clarify it to staff. 2. Create an environment that encourages others to do their best and rewards achievements. 3. Inspire staff to continuously improve.

7. *Implement the coaching plan.* Once the specific action steps are identified and timelines are established, Susan and Don agree on points to check progress. Susan and Don meet every other week and share examples of data Don is implementing. In implementation, Susan utilizes questions and challenges to open space for Don to continue to develop. Examples of Susan's coaching methodologies include:

• Asking direct questions
• Reflecting

- Active listening
- Offering praise and recognition
- Being candid, getting to the point
- Being nonjudgmental
- Being objective
- Challenging assumptions

8. *Reassess and offer feedback.* This reassessment phase is typically integrated into the implementation phase. If mentors are utilized, connection with them is appropriate for integration into the plan. Feedback should be consistent and close to the event that prompts the need for feedback.

In this example Susan is able to provide feedback to Don as she makes direct observation of team meetings and as she observes his staff. Susan talks about her observations and coaches Don to high-level solutions that impact his communication style. Susan also connects with peer mentors who provide direct feedback.

9. *Evaluate.* Evaluation is provided by the manager to gauge the success of the coaching. This phase is necessary to determine whether the developmental need has been met. Some questions that Susan asks Don are:

- What are you doing differently because of our interaction?
- What areas of need do you still want to focus on?
- What help do you need from me?

In addition, Don and Susan discuss the 360° reviews requested at different points in the coaching relationship and data points such as turnover and length of stay.

This evaluation reveals that Don believes the coaching has been a success, but Susan perceives that the skills have not yet been solidified. At this point, Susan focuses on Don's resistance and his readiness to have Susan focus her energy on other employees. Don does overcome his resistance, and continues to focus on action plans.

10. *Create closure.* Success is determined by those engaged in a coaching relationship, both the coach and the coached. Remember, the coachee has the option to succeed or opt out. Susan and Don's outcome is successful because of the established relationship and their shared commitment to success.

Appendix A   Carilion's Scorecard Model

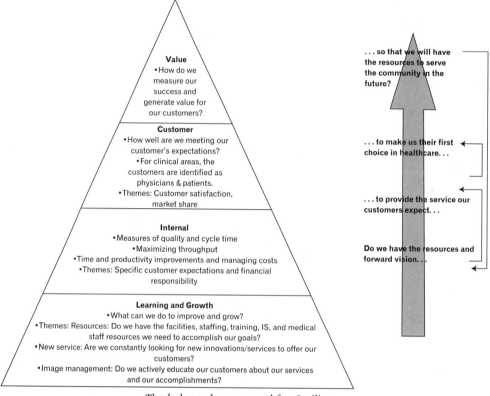

The balanced scorecoard for Carilion.
There is a cause-and-effect relationship between the perspectives.

Appendix B   Carilion's Management Performance Appraisal

Carilion Health System
Level 4 & 5 Performance Appraisal Tool
FY 2005

Name/Title: _____

Reviewer's Name/Title: _____

Evaluation Date: _____ Date: _____ Badge Number: _____

Overall Summary

	Performance Score	×	Performance Weight	=	Overall Score
A. Value Perspective	____	×	____	=	____
Customer Perspective	____	×	____	=	____
Internal Perspective	____	×	____	=	____
Learning and Growth Perspective	____	×	____	=	____
B. Service Standards	____	×	____	=	____
C. Adherence to Policies and Procedures	____	×	____	=	____

Total Performance Evaluation Score:
(Add scores to equal 1.00) ____

Check one:
Significantly exceeds standards (4.5–5.0). ____
Exceeds standards (4.0–4.49). ____
Fully meets standards (3.0–3.99). ____
Meets most standards (2.5–2.99). ____
Does not meet standards (1–2.49). ____

Evaluator Comments: _____

_____

Employee Comments: _____

_____

Employee Signature: _____ Date: _____

Manager Signature: _____ Date: _____

Attach these forms to this summary:
☐ **Continuing Education Record**
☐ **Annual Competency Validation Form (if applicable)**

INSTRUCTIONS

Evaluate the performance of the leader during the past review period according to the criteria outlined in this document. Narrative information is necessary to support numerical ratings indicating Significantly Exceeds Expectations or Needs Significant Improvement.

Rating Scale:
   1—Needs significant improvement.
   3—Meets expectations.
   5—Significantly exceeds expectations.

A.

Value Perspective   **Overall Rating:** _____

Applies key financial concepts and analysis to decision making. Develops and implements actionable work plans with measurable outcomes. Continually assesses and reallocates resources to meet demands.

Competencies to consider in rating performance and developmental goal planning:

- **Financial Acumen.** Understands drivers of financial performance and takes these into account when making decisions.
- **Accountability.** Meets agreed upon commitments
- **Constructive Thinking.** Analyzes problems systematically and logically, and is resourceful in developing and implementing solutions.
- **Process Management.** Develops key initiatives, measures, and targets appropriate to individual business unit. Proactively monitors key performance indicators and adjusts operations to achieve established targets.

Behaviors

Meets expectations:
- Establishes realistic budget using financial and quantitative information.
- Manages budget by monitoring revenue and expenses, takes action to maintain budget and stay within established variances.

- Analyzes data before acting and considers financial impact of decisions.
- Proactively reviews and revises staffing plan to best align human resources against operations, customer demands, and new initiatives.
- Meets margin and scorecard goals.

Significantly exceeds:
- Financial impact has exceeded scorecard goal.
- Implements initiatives with sound financial decisions that impact Carilion Health System's bottom line.
- Utilizes cost/benefit analysis and/or ROI to maximize financial position of business unit.
- Mentoring others in financial acumen.

Achievement of Scorecard Goals/Projects: _____

Developmental Goals for FY '06: _____
_____
_____

Customer Perspective   Overall Rating: _____

Holds self and team accountable for maintaining the highest possible performance standards, serves a diverse group of customers (patients, employees, physicians, colleagues).

Competencies to consider in rating performance and developmental goal planning:

- **Service Orientation and Customer Focus.** Takes customer needs into account when making decisions
- **Building and Strengthening Relationships.** Builds and maintains long-term relationships based on mutual respect and trust, works toward solutions and compromises that consider the needs of all

Behaviors

Meet expectations:
- Customer satisfaction scores reflect continuous performance improvement.
- Promptly resolves patient/customer concerns.

- Role-models customer-focused behaviors for staff.
- Cultivates relationships with stakeholders.

Significantly exceeds:
- Builds coalitions with internal and external customers to advance system initiatives and scorecard goals and to achieve Carilion Health System Mission/Vision.
- Reviews and acts on market data to adjust operations and/or develop new business.
- Continually strives to exceed customer expectations and to be the provider of choice.

Achievement of Scorecard Goals/Projects: ____

Developmental Goals for FY '06: _____

_____

_____

Internal Perspective   Overall Rating: ____

Delivers efficient, consistent, and timely services. Recognizes and acts on opportunities for growth and improvement to advance goals of the organization. Utilizes project management principles to accomplish goals, seeks out appropriate resources, and proactively anticipates change within the market, industry, and healthcare system. Aligns service with the Mission/Vision of the organization. Translates system goals into department specific objectives and priorities.

Competencies to consider in rating performance and developmental goal planning:

- **Project Management.** Implements a formal approach that highlights critical action items, accountabilities, and due dates
- **Performance Improvement.** Understands the business of healthcare, analyzes market trends, benchmarks with others, and makes improvements in internal operations
- **Upward Management.** Regularly updates manager on status of projects, provides information on items of concern to minimize risks and resolve problems
- **Initiative.** Acts on opportunities for growth and advances of the organization, confronts problems quickly

- **Prioritizing and Delegating.** Identifies and implements processes that facilitate delegation and shares responsibility with others
- **Managing Vision and Purpose.** Formulates plan to reflect needs of own area and those of the organization, relates the global vision to daily operations for team, assists with setting of priorities, and provides direction to ensure success.

Behaviors

Meets expectations:
- Demonstrates basic project management skills and meets project expectations.
- Upholds commitments to others.
- Links scorecard metrics to daily operations.
- Streamlines processes to enhance daily operations and customer satisfaction.
- Delegates appropriately for skill match and best outcome.
- Creates actionable work plans for staff in order to achieve goals.

Significantly exceeds:
- Meets or exceeds established scorecard metrics.
- Develops process enhancements that improve patient care and decrease operational costs.
- Creates vision/direction for each business unit.
- Takes initiative to propel business unit toward best in class practice.

Achievement of Scorecard Goals/Projects: _____

Developmental Goals for FY '06: _____
_____
_____

Learning and Growth Perspective   Overall Rating: _____

Inspires enthusiasm and builds support for projects. Attracts, selects, develops, and retains qualified employees, and is effective in utilizing developmental planning to expand employee skills and abilities.

Competencies to consider in rating performance and developmental goal planning:

- **Identifying and Recruiting Talent.** Attracts outstanding staff from diverse backgrounds and fills gaps in team skills and knowledge.
- **Developing and Retaining Talent.** Establishes developmental goals for skill development, offers stretch assignments, provides necessary coaching and education
- **Giving Feedback.** Shares advice and insight on progress toward program goals and objectives, provides performance feedback that is constructive and actionable
- **Communicating Effectively.** Articulates logical arguments, matches communication style of a message to the audience, solicits input from others, expresses ideas clearly, responds to concerns in a timely manner
- **Motivating and Influencing.** Generates commitment and buy-in from a diverse staff on projects.

Behaviors

Meets expectations
- Develops retention plans.
- Consistently follows Carilion's employment process.
- Utilizes interviewing techniques to assess skills and ensure right fit.
- Utilizes resources to develop appropriate orientation process.
- Develops education plans to target gaps in skills and knowledge.
- Accepts accountability for creating environment that fosters retention.
- Utilizes central education dollars based on prioritized needs.
- Creates and maintains dependable methods of communication (monthly staff meetings).
- Uses developmental planning as a tool to meet staff and unit goals.
- Meets established target for turnover rate.
- Utilizes performance management as a tool to develop staff and self.

Significantly exceeds:
- Role-models for and mentors others in recruiting and retaining the most appropriate people.

- Proactively works with HR contacts to support recruitment and development efforts.
- Creates challenging work environment that rewards risk-taking and skill development.
- Implements succession planning and encourages new leaders to emerge.
- Department retention plan offers a variety of recognition methods and strategies to address employee concerns and needs and departmental improvement opportunities; implements, evaluates, and revises routinely.
- Implements coaching and follow-up techniques on employee development; engages employee accountability for improvement.

Achievement of Scorecard Goals/Projects: _____

Developmental Goals for FY '06: _____

_____

_____

B.

Service Standards

Promotes Carilion's Culture of Excellence and quality service through encouraging teamwork; fostering open, honest communication; maintaining a professional environment; respecting others; and anticipating customer needs.

- Teamwork
- Communication
- Physical EnvironmentOverall Rating:
- Respect for Others
- Quality

Overall Rating: _____

Behaviors

Meets expectations: • Anticipates team needs and works cooperatively to accomplish goals together.

- Acknowledges/respects diversity of each team member.
- Is supportive of giving/receiving constructive feedback in a team environment.
- Resolves conflicts privately, taking care not to embarrass or criticize in front of others.
- Utilizes core communication skills effectively.
- Demonstrates honesty and integrity in everyday communication.
- Is accountable for creating positive and productive work environment.
- Respects all aspects of diversity.
- Discourages gossip, rumors, and inappropriate language and behavior.
- Consistently strives to produce a quality product and meet customer expectations.

Exceeds expectations:
- Role-models service standards consistently, coaches others to a higher level of performance.

Comments: _____

1. **360° Feedback (attach summarized feedback) (*if applicable*)**
2. **Required In-services (attach copy)**
3. **Licensure, certifications, CMEs, etc. (attach copies)**
4. **Leader Comments:** _____
   _____
   _____

5. **Signatures:**

   Employee _____ Date _____

   Reviewer _____ Date _____

PERFORMANCE PLAN

Progress on current performance-period goals and action plans:				
	Achieved		Continue During Next Performance Period	
Goals	Yes	No	Yes	No

Developmental goals and action plans for next performance period: Growth needs to occur to obtain the goal.
Developmental Goal:
Action Steps:
Developmental Goal:
Action Steps:
Operational Goals: Assumption is that no development is needed to obtain the goals.
Career Goals:

Managers are knowledgeable and accountable for utilization of policies and procedures that direct Carilion Health Systems processes, and they are accountable for providing educational resources to employees on policy and procedure utilizaiton.

Appendix C   Action Plan

1. Carilion's Performance Plan Process
2. Carilion's Performance Planning Document
3. Example of Performance Plan with Operational and Developmental Examples

1. Carilion's Performance Plan Process

As a performance is discussed at the annual review, it often becomes apparent that additional skill development is required or desirable. Employee performance has demonstrated that there is a need for improved skills or that the employee is ready to take on additional responsibilities that require knowledge and skill acquisitions.

A performance plan is a tool that guides the individual as she strives for personal and professional growth. The plan should assist the employee in enhancing areas that need improvement and in developing new competencies.

The performance plan is developed jointly between employee and manager. Goals are established and action steps are identified that will guide the employee in meeting the goals.

When readying employees for their annual performance appraisal, the manager should encourage them to come to the review prepared to discuss their performance

After completing the performance appraisal tool, utilize the performance plan to guide the process.

Step 1: Review goals from the previous year. Determine whether these goals were achieved. If they were not achieved, evaluate whether they are still current for the upcoming year.

Step 2: Be sure that goals are *smart*. Goals can be short range or long range. Goals with time frames are easier to measure and to evaluate. The more specific a goal is, the easier it is to develop an action plan to meet the goal. Goals should be thought of as a "statement of intent." Goals should be written with regard to employee's performance and behaviors. Once you have transferred any goals that are being carried over from the most recent performance period, identify additional areas that need improvement. Look first to see whether there are any significant responsibilities that received a rating of "Needs Improvement." These need to be incorporated into the plan so that the employee will focus on meeting the expectations for this job responsibility by the next performance appraisal. Next, look to any new responsibilities the employee is ready to assume. Is there a need for training and developing? If so, build this education into performance plan.

Step 3: Identify the action steps that will assist the employee in meeting the goal. Again, this should be done jointly. The manager is responsible for guiding this process and helping the employee identify available resources; however, the employee needs to be a part of this plan in order to "buy in." The action steps should be thought of as ways to accomplish the goal. Action steps should include, but are not limited to, activities, resources, and time frames.

Step 4: Follow up on action plans. Check with employee to see that she is completing the action steps. Assess what kind of assistance she may need or whether it is necessary to revise action plan. New circumstances may have developed that are impacting the developmental plan. Document any action taken to reflect the status of the developmental plan.

2. Carilion's Performance Planning Document

PERFORMANCE PLAN

Progress on current performance-period goals and action plans:				
	Achieved		Continue During Next Performance Period	
Goals	Yes	No	Yes	No

Developmental goals and action plans for next performance period: Growth needs to occur to obtain the goal.
Developmental Goal:
Action Steps:
Developmental Goal:
Action Steps:
Operational Goals: Assumption is that no development is needed to obtain the goals.
Career Goals:

3. Example of Performance Plan with Operational and Developmental Examples

I.	Scorecard:	Value/Growth Increase financials through M&A growth
	Operational Goal:	Design and implement M&A plan
	Assumption:	Proficient in skills
	Developmental Goal:	Develop M&A knowledge

Action Steps

1. Research and understand M&A processes. Develop education plan for self, share with director, and implement plan.
2. Relate M&A process to HRD functions.
3. Develop M&A project plan for HRD functions.
4. Seek feedback from director regarding the plan.
5. Implement and evaluate the plan.

Assumption: Needs development
Outcome: Both operational and developmental goals end with the same outcomes.

II. Scorecard: Value
                      Meet financial goals

Operational Goal: Meet financial goals

Action Steps

1. Increase revenue.
2. Decrease costs.
3. Decrease overtime.

Assumption: Proficient in skills
Developmental Goal: Meet financial goals by expanding health-care knowledge related to finance.

Action Steps

1. Develop relationships with financial adviser to gain knowledge of adviser role.
2. Analyze and react to financial reports.
3. Identify, monitor, and actively promote cost containment methods. Seek feedback from director.
4. Attend education-related budget methods.
5. Complete budget independently.

Appendix D Carilion's Formal Coaching Definition, Model, and Process

1. Carilion's coaching definition
2. Carilion's coaching model
3. Carilion's coaching process

1. Carilion's Coaching Definition

Carilion defines coaching as an active process that promotes and brings about change in an individual's thoughts, attitudes, and behaviors related to agreed-upon performance expectations.

2. Carilion's Coaching Model

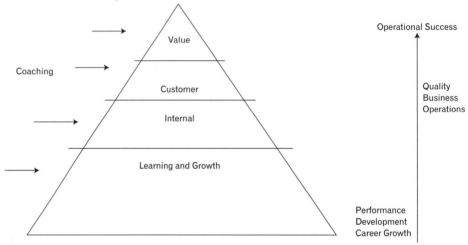

3. Carilion's Coaching Process

1. Establish the need (review and performance plan).
2. Create a relationship.
3. Evaluate readiness for change.
4. Determine commitment to coaching.
5. Use discovery and observation.
6. Establish the plan: specific action strategies.
7. Implement the coaching plan.
8. Reassess and offer feedback.
9. Evaluate.
10. Create closure.

Be aware of and ready to deal with resistance during any phase.

CHAPTER 10

Notes from the Field

Philosophy, Principles, and Approaches from
Various Organizations

The Accenture Philosophy

CAROLYN HENNING, EMPLOYEE ENGAGEMENT AND ENABLEMENT PRODUCTS CAPABILITY
TEAM, CHICAGO, ILLINOIS

Accenture is a global management consulting, technology services, and outsourcing company with net revenues of US$13.67 billion for the fiscal year ended August 31, 2004.

As a professional service company, Accenture sees its employees as its product, so the company focuses on developing staff in the areas of value creator, people developer, and business operator. The company recognizes that value is created for its clients by high performers who produce desired outcomes better than those of the competition. High performers want their contribution to be very visible and to work in an environment that enables even higher performance.

Scale and complexity are Accenture's main challenges. With more than 110,000 people in forty-eight countries and four distinctive workforces, creating a high-performing work environment requires discipline and innovative approaches. Performance management at Accenture is focused on developing this environment by creating a universal language for talking about performance; processes for ensuring that performance is measured against simple, common, and global standards; a climate that fosters performance transparency; and consequences that are aligned to demonstrated outcomes. At Accenture, the goal is to develop individual capability in order to improve individual performance and, in turn, drive aggregate company performance.

While meritocracy is the cornerstone of Accenture's performance management philosophy, this philosophy is adapted to the needs of its four workforces so that the model is either "up or out" or position-based. For all workforces, the height of the bar is defined and then calibrated each year.

Accenture sells the capability of its employees, so the development of that capability is a critical pillar of the company's career framework. Creating a high-performing work environment requires seamless integration of performance management, rewards, and professional development.

Professional development at Accenture comprises three components: *guidance and feedback*, which includes input from leaders and individuals regarding performance; *experiences*, which includes roles and assignments, daily tasks, challenges, and problems; and *support*, which includes formal training, knowledge, coaching, and other performance support. To be successful, Accenture's employees need to manage each of these areas carefully.

Accenture builds its employees' skills in an innovative way. While the four workforces differ, each has a relatively consistent curriculum framework. The framework ensures that all Accenture people develop skills in the following areas:

- *Core Professional Skills*. These skills are common across jobs and roles and define the Accenture professional. They include interpersonal skills, business skills, and skills that embody Accenture's culture.
- *Specialty Skills*. These skills are in a specific technical or functional area. They ensure that Accenture's employees remain market-relevant and able to deliver high-quality business solutions within Accenture and to Accenture's clients.
- *Industry Skills* (where applicable). These skills and knowledge revolve around the way Accenture's clients do business in the various industries that Accenture serves.
- *Job Readiness Skills*. These skills are required to enable individuals to perform a specific role or set of tasks.

Each workforce has a different set of skills in each of these areas. In addition, each focuses its investment in these areas differently. However, thanks to the use of a consistent framework, all employees at Accenture are given the opportunity to develop both long-term professional skills and short-term, job-specific skills.

Accenture's performance management process provides feedback and guidance on both professional skills and job-specific skills to help individuals acquire and demonstrate increasing levels of capability.

Managing Performance

STEPHEN GLEN, POLLAK LEARNING ALLIANCE, SYDNEY, AUSTRALIA

Pollak Learning Alliance has created a performance management system that provides the following outcomes:

1. Reviews each employee's performance in relation to key accountabilities
2. Allows the employee and her manager to create a plan for future training needs and aspirations.

This second outcome of the performance management process is administered through Personal Development Plans, which are created biannually. Information on the process is provided in the following sections.

Stage 1: Performance Planning

Performance planning is the process of setting performance goals in relation to the key accountabilities associated with your role.

Commonly, setting performance goals involves having an understanding of your key accountabilities, setting goals in relation to these accountabilities, and deciding how you will measure the achievement of your goals. This process is performed collaboratively with your manager. Through this process you will agree upon your key accountabilities as documented in your role and responsibility statement and discuss what achievements can be reasonably expected given employees' current level of performance and training requirements. (See Figure 10-1.)

Figure 10-1. Stage 1: Performance planning (establishing accountabilities, KPIs, and goals).

Name: _____   Manager: _____

Position: _____   Location: _____

Department: _____   Review Period: _____

Determining Accountabilities, KPIs, and Goals
- Key accountabilities will be derived from the role and responsibility statement (RRS) and should be agreed to through team or individual consultation with the manager.
- KPIs will be determined through team or individual consultation with the manager.
- Goals will be determined on an individual basis in consultation between the manager and the candidate.

Key Accountabilities	KPIs (measures)	Goals/Targets (for 6-month period)

Stage 2: Performance Reviews

Performance reviews are the keystone of our performance management process and are vital in the ongoing development of our staff. The management team is committed to ensuring that these reviews occur regularly for all our staff.

A performance review is a formal meeting between each staff member and his manager. These meetings are held twice a year, usually in December or January and in June or July. The success of these meetings is dependent on both parties' communicating and working together effectively.

Performance reviews provide the opportunity for:

- Two-way discussion (50/50)
- Measuring your achieved performance against goals and key performance indicators (KPIs)
- Identifying action plan in those areas that can be improved

The manager and staff member complete the Performance Management Form (see Figure 10-2) prior to attending this meeting and come prepared to discuss their individual perspectives. We encourage open

Figure 10-2. Stage 2: Performance review.

Part I: General Accomplishments (to be completed by candidate)

List your major accomplishments during this period. (Provide examples; be specific.)	What areas do you feel you need improvement in? (Provide examples; be specific.)
What new skills have you developed during this period?	**Comment on your contribution to the PLA. values (Provide examples; be specific.)**

Part 2: Review of Goals

1. Goals are copied and pasted from Stage 1 of the form.
2. Manager and candidate discuss results during the review period (manager to provide evidence of results).
3. Manager and candidate discuss and assign the rating in a collaborative effort. (This should be based on objective performance criteria.)
4. Manager and candidate consider areas for improvement (these will be used in Stage 3).

Rating Scale:

SAT—Significantly Above Target
AT—Above Target
OT—On Target
BT—Below Target

Goals (targets)	Results during period	Rating Scale				Areas for further development
		SAT	AT	OT	BT	

and respectful communication during this meeting so that a productive outcome is reached and agreed to by both parties.

The information discussed in this meeting is recorded in our employee database. The only people who will have access to this information are the staff member, his manager, and HR.

Stage 3: Personal Development Plans

Once the performance review has been completed, the staff member is required to consider her personal goals and actions for the next six months. This is documented in what is known as a personal development plan (see Figure 10-3).

Principles

- Provide all employees with the opportunity to set goals in relation to their personal and professional development needs.
- Where possible, align individual goals to the business objectives.

Figure 10-3. Stage 3: Personal development plan.

Part 1: Fill in the table to create your personal development plan.

Candidate will determine action plan and support requirements and gain approval of manager.

Development Objectives (agreed during review)	Action Plan (include time frames)		Support Required	Approval
	Possible Action (please detail)	Time Frame		

Part 2: Commitment to Objectives

The goals, action plans, and support arrangements are agreed to for the following performance period.

Period (6 months); _____   Today's Date: _____

Manager's
Signature: _____   Employee's
Signature: _____

- Provide support, feedback and encouragement throughout the process.
- Ensure the commitment and involvement of all employees in the process.
- Identify training requirements.

A Performance Management System

DANA PATRICK AND CARLYN HOUSTON, ARMY AIR FORCE EXCHANGE SERVICE (AAFES)

The Army Air Force Exchange Service (AAFES) adopted a new performance management system in 2003 that strives to develop a competent and skilled workforce by establishing companywide performance standards in a people-oriented structure. This performance management system combines industry best practices and a four-phase performance management model with cutting-edge technology to provide associates top-down direction for their work and corporate support for their learning and development.

Under this system, the performance management process begins when AAFES sets the corporate goals for the year. Then, associates set goals that support the corporate goals. They use their division's goals, their supervisor's goals, and three to five performance drivers (job-specific parameters) to aid in the goal-setting process. Associates must also rate themselves as "area for development," "solid skill," or "clear strength" on the fifteen management leadership competencies (skill sets related to how goals are accomplished). When the performance cycle ends and it is time for the performance evaluation, associates are rated on both their goals and their competencies, with more weight given to the competencies.

Associates are encouraged to view performance management as more than goal setting and performance evaluations. They are reminded that performance management is a continuous process with four phases. The process begins by planning and goal setting; clarifying responsibilities, requirements, and expectations; performing; and developing associates early in the performance cycle (Phase 1: Planning). The process continues as the manager monitors progress and provides support through feedback and coaching while the associate performs and develops throughout the year (Phase 2: Performing). Then, the performance management process flows into a summary evaluation of results and skills at the end of the performance cycle (Phase 3: Performance Review). The end of the performance cycle provides the foundation for the performance goals and development plans in the next year (Phase 4: Development Planning).

This four-phase model is reinforced by AAFES's electronic performance management system. Associates enter their goals and competency ratings into an Electronic Performance Goal Worksheet (EPGW). The system is designed so that the associate and the supervisor are encouraged to discuss the associate's EPGW before the supervisor approves it. As the performance cycle progresses, associates can return to their EPGW and update their goals as necessary. When updates are completed, associates can send their EPGW back to their supervisor for more discussion before approval. There is also an Electronic Individual Career Development Plan (EICDP) associated with the EPGW. The EICDP is connected with the fifteen management leadership competencies and helps associates identify learning opportunities that address their areas for development.

AAFES's performance management system was designed to emphasize workforce competency by establishing companywide performance standards and a people-oriented structure. Even though a pay increase can be a result of the performance management process, the purpose of performance management is to ensure that associates have the necessary skills to meet AAFES's corporate goals.

Seven Coaching Principles

HOLLY BURKETT, EVALUATION WORKS, DAVIS, CALIFORNIA

One of the best coaching experiences I've ever had occurred during my participation as a Team in Training (TNT) member with The Leukemia and Lymphoma Society. Signing up to run my first marathon was both an exhilarating and intimidating venture, and I wasn't at all sure I could go the distance of twenty-six miles, give up a regular diet of Krispy Kremes for a structured workout schedule, or meet my aggressive fundraising targets. But a wonderful thing happened—I was introduced to a personal coach who gave me the inspiration, training, and confidence to achieve what seemed to be then an impossible goal.

My coach, Robert Kane, and other enthusiastic TNT coaches, infused their protégés with the joy of running and all its physical, mental, and lifestyle benefits. They freely shared information, resources, and lessons learned. They relayed a vision of the leukemia or lymphoma patients who were depending upon our efforts. A bracelet with our patient's name was a tangible, enduring symbol that we were running for something larger than ourselves. Our coaches provided a series of short-term, achievable goals, each geared to individuals' different fitness levels. They emphasized slow and steady progress, not speed or perfection. They boosted confidence and cheered every time a new milestone was met. They cautioned against the dangers of hitting a plateau, burning out, or expecting too much from yourself. We were encouraged to challenge ourselves yet have fun with our workouts, partner with others, and take time to rest and rebuild. We were expected to succeed, and we did.

In any organization, the best coaches follow similar principles for guiding others to meet individual or strategic goals:

1. *Stress personal motivators.* Employees' energy and commitment to performance improvement are driven by individual goals, interests, and desires. An effective coach asks questions about employees' ambitions, dreams, and experiences.

2. *Use visioning.* Align employees' picture of their desired future with the organization's image of success. Show employees how their work performance matters in the bigger scheme of things.

3. *Establish goals.* Specific, achievable, relevant goals provide direction, clarity, and a framework for measuring progress.

4. *Create development plans.* An action-oriented development plan provides collaborative opportunities to maximize strengths and to grow in areas needing improvement. Organizations that invest in employees' development are those that attract and retain the best talent.

5. *Strive for excellence.* Emphasize excellence and provide standards by which to gauge progress and thresholds of achievement.

6. *Provide necessary resources.* Information, tools, and resources are needed to support employees' success in achieving performance or developmental goals. An effective coach recognizes enablers to employees' success and is willing to anticipate and remove potential barriers.

7. *Recognize accomplishments.* Whether running in a marathon or climbing rungs in a corporate ladder, individuals cannot expect to see immediate results. It can be fatiguing to continually fine-tune physical,

emotional, and intellectual muscles in order to go the distance. Praise and recognition for small wins boost self-esteem and give employees the confidence to keep channeling and challenging their capabilities.

Ultimately, an organization's ability to survive and thrive in today's economy hinges on how well it maximizes and leverages its pool of human capital. There can be no organizational results without individual results. Effective coaching, then, is a powerful way to help position employees as managers of their own career and the chief architects of a high-performing workplace.

Manager as Coach

SUSAN KIRKPATRICK MUEHLBACH, LEADERSHIP AND MANAGEMENT DEVELOPMENT (A LEGAL PUBLISHING COMPANY)

One of the roles managers play each day is that of a coach. They are required to deliver business results through people. The direct reports of each manager are the players on the field. The manager is the coach on the sidelines. In many cases, the manager used to be a player. This makes the role as a coach difficult in some ways. In his old role, the manager was accountable for individual results. Now the manager must work through people to accomplish results.

There are three major ways a manager can coach: coaching to expectations, coaching to the motivation of the individual performer, and coaching to performance. They are all intertwined but sometimes require different skills.

Coaching to Expectations

In order to coach to expectations, the manager must lay out clear expectations beforehand. This can be done at performance review time or during another business cycle throughout the year. In the world of sales managers, the expectations are very clear: meet or exceed your sales quota.

The manager works with each sales representative to determine how to meet that expectation. The manager uses various tools to help the rep meet the quota. This includes analysis tools for a particular territory or customer base, forecasting tools, market data, and the rep's individual style in prospecting, cold calling, and making appointments.

In the end, the only thing that matters is whether a sale is made. A strong manager will use all resources available to her to ensure that the rep understands expectations and has the support and resources to make the sale.

Coaching to Motivation

Being a sales representative in a 100 percent commission job is challenging and rewarding. In our company, the reps work from their homes and are often located hundreds of miles from their peers and managers. If a rep in our business is not self-motivated, she will soon be looking for a job that is a better fit. The challenge for the manager is to discover what motivates each rep and to coach to that motivation. By the sheer nature of the job, most people do not have the interest or skills to succeed in such a high-pressure position. However, for those with the knowledge, skills, and abilities, sales can be a long-term rewarding career.

However, even the best reps find themselves in a slump once in a while. This situation presents the opportunity for the manager to diagnose the problem and to offer support. The better the manager knows his rep, the sooner he is able to coach to the motivation of that particular rep.

Coaching to Performance

The ultimate challenge and responsibility of the manager is to coach to maximum performance. She should use all of the tools, resources, support, and ideas of peers and direct reports to coach the employee to performance.

Coaching to performance is difficult if clear expectations are not set and presented in a way that leads to understanding on the part of both the manager and the rep. In the world of our sales reps, performance is a reflection of the ability to meet or exceed quota. In other industries and professions, performance may be more difficult to define.

What does it look like if someone is performing? What does it look like if someone is *not* performing? The manager needs to ensure that clear expectations are set and managed.

Sometimes employees understand expectations but are not performing due to motivation issues. Perhaps they are going through a difficult time in their personal lives. The manager needs to ask appropriate questions to discover what the gaps are between motivation and performance and then do what she can to close the gap.

Being a manager can be challenging and rewarding. A manager needs to understand both the business she is involved in and the individuals who report to her. The daily challenge of the manager is to work through the direct reports to ensure that company goals are met. This is an ongoing process and requires skills, knowledge, and motivation to accomplish consistently.

Coach as Facilitator

CATHY BOLGER, OWNER, EMPLOYEE DEVELOPMENT, SAN DIEGO, CALIFORNIA

In the book *Coaching Training*, the author, Chris Chen, presents four facets of coaching: coach as guide, coach as motivator, coach as teacher, and coach as mentor.[1] In other words, the effective coach must, given differing situations, be able to move fluidly among coaching approaches.

Many managers, however, are tempted to give quick advice. It is often easier to tell coachees/team members what to think and what to do. According to the authors of *Crucial Confrontations*, we don't even think about it.[2] We are experienced and we understand how things work. It's positively Pavlovian. We see a problem, and the gate is up and our tongues are off and running.

Sometimes, providing an answer is entirely appropriate, especially if time frames are very short and a situation has high priority. However, giving answers and advice can actually get in the way of effective coachee development. Indeed, many managers may see their jobs as simply telling their staffs who reports what and how to do something.

However, when the coach is guiding a coachee toward growth and empowerment, the coach as guide may be the best choice. The coach-as-guide approach is a process based on allowing coachees to come to their own conclusions and solutions.

One assumption when choosing to guide rather than tell is that the answer lies within the coachee. As John Whitmore writes in his book *Coaching for Performance*, "The coachee does acquire the facts, not from the coach, but within himself, stimulated by the coach. The coach thus encourages coachees to work from their own experiences and perceptions."[3]

The model I present here is from Whitmore's book. There are four

steps, spelling out GROW: Goal (of the session), Reality (currently happening), Options (in the coach's view), Will (action coachee will take).
Here are some questions a coach might ask:

1. Goal for Session
   • What would you like to get out of this session?
   • What would be most helpful for you to take away from this session?
   • What do you want to achieve?
   • What role do you want me to play in this session?
2. Reality
   • What action have you taken so far?
   • What were the effects of that action?
   • What are the major constraints to moving forward?
3. Options
   • Let's list the options you see at this point.
   • What else could you do?
   • What if:
     —Budget is not a factor?
     —You had more staff?
     —You had a magic wand and could do anything you wanted?
4. Will
   • What will you do?
   • When will you do it?
   • Will it meet your goal?
   • What obstacles might you meet?
   • What support do you need?

Another advantage of using a guided approach to coaching is well stated by Bob Pike, author of *Creative Training Techniques*: People don't argue with their own data.[4] They may however, argue with yours. So when you decide that a guided coaching process is best, give the GROW model a try.

References
1. Chris W. Chen, *Coaching Training* (Alexandria, Va.: ASTD Press, 2003).
2. Kerry Patterson, Joseph Grenny, Ron McMillan, and Al Switzler, *Crucial Confrontations* (New York: McGraw-Hill, 2005).
3. John Whitmore, *Coaching for Performance* (London: Nicholas Berkley, 2002).

4. Robert Pike, *Creative Training Techniques Handbook: Tips, Tactics, and How-To's for Delivering Effective Training,* 2nd ed. (Minneapolis, Lakewood Publications, 1994).

Coaching Managers Through the Appraisal Process

RITA LAITRES, HUMAN RELATIONS SPECIALIST, COLORADO DIVISION OF WILDLIFE AND OWNER, DYNAMIC CONSULTING SERVICES, BOULDER, COLORADO

Many managers view performance appraisals as distasteful and something to avoid at all cost. But what *is* the cost of glossing over a managerial job duty required by most employers? Do managers in your organization receive the proper training, coaching, and feedback before they embark on what may be perceived as an unpleasant task?

If your answer is anything other than a resounding yes, invest a few minutes to review the following techniques to transform your organization's performance evaluation process into an employee development asset.

> Just as we wouldn't give someone a dangerous tool without providing safety training, human resource professionals must train and coach managers to use performance management tools effectively—and, in this case, performance appraisals.

Performance management training *is critical* to your organization. Many organizations fail to provide their managers with the proper training to perform employee evaluations.

Model: Training, Coaching, and Continuous Feedback

Training: Providing managers with a meaningful learning experience is an invaluable service to your managers and employees.

Training Activities

- Reframe the evaluation process for your managers: Performance evaluation is not a once-a-year event; rather, evaluation is an essential tool in the performance management process.
- Adopt a results-driven performance process that increases employees' overall performance and ultimately impacts the organization's bottom line.

- Present a model stressing the continuous cycle of communication, evaluation, action planning, and *tangible* outcomes.
- Stress that a tool not used properly can do more harm than good.
- An effective performance evaluation process allows the manager and the employee to jointly develop a *work product* that clarifies performance expectations, establishes short-term and long-term goals, and creates an action plan for development or improvement.

Coaching: Training is only the first step. Without coaching, your organization may lose a chance to capitalize on managers' learning experiences. There's no value in the learning experience if managers *never* transfer newly gained skills and knowledge to the job. Coaching is the impetus to move the learning activity from the classroom to the workplace.

> Coaching managers through the performance evaluation process significantly reduces their stress level and makes the process a positive and productive experience for managers and employees.

Coaching Activities

- Understand their anxiety, and be empathic. Just as many of us are nervous about practicing a new skill, managers may also be apprehensive about adopting and implementing new concepts. Old habits die hard and are more comfortable than venturing into unfamiliar territory.
- Build trusting relationships. Managers will share their feelings and opinions with you, and it is important to maintain confidentiality. Above all, it's critical for managers to know that their conversations will remain private.
- Offer encouragement, support, and praise often and early into the process. *Positive reinforcement* is a powerful technique to reward desired outcomes. Never underestimate the value of positive and constructive feedback.
- Provide managers with the opportunity to *privately* practice their new skills with you. Create a safe environment. There's a reason every acting company does a dress rehearsal—it's an opportunity to iron out the kinks before the real performance.
- Role-model the behavior for your managers. Coaching is similar to performance evaluation components: communicate, clarify expectations, enhance performance, and link action plans to business goals.

Continuous Feedback: The third concept of the model is continual and constructive feedback. This element, similar to baseball's "clean-up" batter in the lineup, produces results and scores runs. Feedback breathes energy into the process and encourages managers to stick with it instead of bailing out.

Continuous Feedback Activities

- Include a self-appraisal component to allow managers to judge their progress. This self-evaluation allows you and the manager to discuss similarities and differences in the two assessments.
- Encourage managers to keep the process alive and build on momentum. Send e-mails or write articles in your company newsletter to reinforce concepts.
- Remind managers to proactively manage their employees' performance. The concept of continual feedback recognizes accomplishments on a timely basis and resolves concerns before they develop into serious performance issues.
- Hold your managers accountable for actively participating in the performance management process. The evaluation process is a tool to monitor and validate individual performance and contributions; however, if the tool is not used regularly, it begins to rust and lose its effectiveness.
- Collect testimonials and, with permission, share these wins with other managers. Success breeds success.

The model is designed to transform the performance appraisal process from a dreaded annual activity to a positive process to enhance individual and organizational success. Would a wise manager pass on a sure bet?

Example:
Continuous Feedback Memo

To: Managers
From: Company President
      and VP of HR

RE: Performance Management—You hold the key to your employee's success

As you prepare for discussions with your employees, ask yourself the following questions and let your answers guide the performance appraisal process:

1. What do I need to say or do to capitalize on my employees' skills and talents?
2. What assignments will motivate my employees to produce stellar results?
3. How will I explain how their accomplishments contribute to their performances?

C H A P T E R   1 1

Sample Forms

n this chapter, I have gathered a number of performance appraisal forms that come from many types and sizes of organizations. (The names of the specific organizations have been taken off the forms.) They also reflect many different approaches to appraising employee performance, and you may find it helpful to compare them.

Each form or set of forms is preceded by my observations on its strong and weak features. As you study the forms, look for ideas that you can use or adapt. Keep in mind the following criteria:

1. The forms must accomplish your objectives.
2. They must be successfully communicated and sold to those who will use them.
3. Your organization must be able to handle the paperwork.
4. The forms should be useful both for clarifying what's expected and for appraising performance.
5. They should result in improved performance on the part of the employee.
6. They should help to maintain rapport between manager and employee.

Example 1

Instead of establishing standards ahead of time, appraisers are asked to describe the employee's status regarding each factor. This invites a great deal of subjective evaluation even though the form suggests that judgment should be based on facts and figures whenever possible.

Too much writing is required. It would be better to have ratings with possible comments to explain them. Also, the last question is too subjective to be of any value. ("Is there understanding and acceptance of standards to measure future performance?")

The overall performance rating symbols stand for:

I = Incompetent	S = Satisfactory
Cd = Conditional	C = Commendable
M = Marginal	O = Outstanding

PERFORMANCE APPRAISAL
Salaried Nonexempt Employees

This Review Date

Last Review Date

Next Review Date

Name _____ Dept _____ Serial _____

Position _____ Code _____

Employment Date _____ Birth Date _____ Date Assigned Position _____

Is this position correct? Yes____ No____ If no, explain _____

_____

Give a clear concise statement identifying employee's status regarding each of the factors below. Judgment should be based on facts and figures whenever possible.

Production: Volume of work performed.

_____

_____

_____

_____

Quality: Quality of work performed, including cost.

_____

_____

_____

_____

Initiative and Ingenuity: Ability to decide and take proper action outside the area of specific instructions.

_____

_____

_____

_____

_____

Dependability: Acceptance of responsibility; reliability; a realistic approach to assignments and problems.

_____

_____

_____

_____

(continues)

Attendance/Promptness: Absenteeism, tardiness.

_____
_____
_____

Relationships: Cooperation with and attitude toward others.

_____
_____
_____

Knowledge: Possession of knowledge available to performance of the job.

_____
_____
_____

Significant Area(s) of Improvement Since Last Appraisal

_____
_____
_____

Significant Area(s) for Improvement

_____
_____
_____

Is there understanding and acceptance of standards to measure future performance?

Yes   No

PERFORMANCE RATING   ☐ I   ☐ Cd   ☐ M   ☐ S   ☐ C   ☐ O

RATING PRIMARILY BASED ON: ☐ Performance   ☐ Progress

SIGNATURES:

Supervisor: _____ Position _____ Date _____
Supervisor's
Supervisor: _____ Position _____ Date _____

Employee: _____ Date _____

This signature confirms that an interview took place.
It does not necessarily imply agreement.

Example 2

For a simple form, this has some good features. It has been designed for a specific job (sales) and excludes sales volume, which is evaluated in objective terms.

Five major segments have been identified. After each one, each rating is explained instead of described in general rating words such as *outstanding* or *satisfactory*. It also encourages examples and comments.

Another positive feature is the requirement to identify strengths and areas to improve. It also asks for suggestions regarding training or experience to make the individual a more valuable employee. This is far short of a performance improvement plan but goes further than most forms do in considering ways to improve performance.

This form lends itself nicely to self-appraisal.

SALES PERFORMANCE EVALUATION

(OTHER THAN SALES VOLUME)

SALESPERSON'S NAME _____   TIME ON THIS JOB _____ _____
                                                                                       (years)   (months)

EVALUATOR'S NAME _____   DATE THIS
                                                REPORT COMPLETED _____

ITEM TO BE EVALUATED	FOR EACH ITEM ON LEFT, PLEASE CHECK STATEMENT BELOW THAT MOST ACCURATELY DESCRIBES WORK, AND GIVE ACTUAL EXAMPLES OR COMMENTS AS TO WORK PERFORMANCE.			
1 CUSTOMER SERVICE	GIVES CUSTOMER PROMPT AND EFFECTIVE SERVICE. BUILDS VOLUME THROUGH GOOD SERVICE. ☐	SERVICE TO CUSTOMER IS GENERALLY SATISFACTORY. ☐	SOME IMPROVEMENT NEEDED IN HANDLING SERVICE. ☐	SERVICE TO CUSTOMER IS UNSATISFACTORY. ☐
	Examples/Comments:			
2 TERRITORIAL COVERAGE	OUTSTANDING COVERAGE, TRIPS PLANNED WITH EXCEL-LENT REGARD FOR COST OF TRAVEL RELATIVE TO POTENTIAL OF CUSTOMER. ☐	GOOD COVERAGE, TRIPS USUALLY WELL PLANNED AS TO FREQUENCY IN RELATION TO CUSTOMER POTENTIAL AND COST. ☐	SOME IMPROVEMENT NEEDED. COVERAGE FAIR AND NOT AS WELL PLANNED AS IT SHOULD BE. ☐	MUCH IMPROVEMENT NEEDED. COVERAGE IS INADEQUATE. ☐
	Examples/Comments:			
3 EXPENSE CONTROL	USES EXPENSE ACCOUNT WISELY AND WITH INTEG-RITY. EXCEPTIONALLY CAREFUL AND EFFECTIVE USE OF EXPENSE ACCT. ☐	USUALLY USES GOOD JUDGEMENT IN HANDLING EXPENSES. ☐	SOMETIMES MAKES UN-WISE USE OF EXPENSE ACCOUNT IN THE MATTER OF TELEPHONE CALLS, ENTERTAINMENT OR OTHER CHARGES. ☐	ABUSES EXPENSE AC-COUNT, REQUIRES FRE-QUENT CRITICISM. ☐
	Examples/Comments:			
4 REPORTS AND RECORDS	ALL RECORDS AND RE-PORTS UP-TO-DATE AND ON TIME. RECORDS AND REPORTS ARE COMPLETE AND ACCURATE. ☐	REPORTS AND RECORDS ARE GENERALLY ON TIME, UP-TO-DATE, AND COM-PLETE. ☐	SOME IMPROVEMENT NEEDED. ☐	LATE, INADEQUATE, OR IN-COMPLETE REPORTS AND RECORDS. ☐
	Examples/Comments:			
5 KNOWLEDGE OF PRODUCTS, PRICES AND POLICIES	UNUSUALLY WELL IN-FORMED. KEEPS ABREAST OF NEW PRODUCTS, POLICIES, AND REQUIRE-MENTS. ☐	GOOD GENERAL UNDER-STANDING OF PRODUCTS, PRICES, AND POLICIES. ☐	NEED FOR SOME IM-PROVEMENT INDICATED. SOME BUSINESS MAY BE LOST BECAUSE OF LACK OF KNOWLEDGE. ☐	INADEQUATE KNOWLEDGE. INSUFFI-CIENT EFFORT TO LEARN. ☐
	Examples/Comments:			

ANSWER THE FOLLOWING QUESTIONS FULLY:

What various things does this individual do especially well? _____
_____
_____
_____

In what respects does this individual need to improve? _____
_____
_____
_____

What added training or experience would make this individual a more valuable employee? _____
_____
_____
_____

What is this individual's all-around job performance? *(Please check the statement that best describes your appraisal.)*

DESCRIPTION OF ALL-AROUND JOB PERFORMANCE	CHECK
1. One of the best performers.	☐
2. A good performer.	☐
3. A satisfactory performer	☐
4. Some improvement needed to become satisfactory	☐
5. Much improvement needed to become satisfactory	☐

REMARKS _____
_____
_____
_____
_____
_____
_____
_____
_____
_____

REPORT PREPARED BY _____ DATE _____

REPORT REVIEWED BY _____ DATE _____

RECORD OF INTERVIEW: This report was discussed with the incumbent

BY _____   _____
(SIGNATURE)   (DATE)

Example 3

Again, for a simple form, this has some good features. Eight major factors have been selected. Although standards have not been developed, each rating is explained. In order to encourage objectivity on the part of the appraiser, major weak points as well as strong points of the employee are required.

The form's major weakness is the lack of specifics regarding improved performance. One question asks what further training would be helpful, but this is inadequate to accomplish the objective of improved performance.

This type of form also works well for a self-appraisal.

EMPLOYEE PERFORMANCE RATING				DATE DUE	

EMPLOYEE NO.	NAME		SERVICE DATE	LABOR GRADE	JOB CLASSIFICATION

PROBATION MONTH	PROBATION END	ANNUAL	SEMIANNUAL	SPECIAL	PERIOD COVERED	RATING

FACTORS	UNSATISFACTORY					MARGINAL					GOOD					VERY GOOD					EXCELLENT				
	1	2	3	4	5	6	7	8	9	10	11	12	13	14	15	16	17	18	19	20	21	22	23	24	25

1. QUALITY OF WORK

Disregard volume. Consider only whether work is accurate, neat, thorough.

No Opportunity To Observe ☐

UNSATISFACTORY	MARGINAL	GOOD	VERY GOOD	EXCELLENT
Work is very slipshod with frequent and avoidable errors.	Makes frequent errors; work is often careless.	Work is generally satisfactory. Occasionally uncorrected errors slip through.	Work is almost always accurate and neat; corrects errors himself.	Work is always of superior quality.

Remarks:

2. COOPERATIVENESS

Consider attitude toward work, associates, and company; willingness to work for and with others; readiness to give new ideas and methods a fair trial.

No Opportunity To Observe ☐

UNSATISFACTORY	MARGINAL	GOOD	VERY GOOD	EXCELLENT
Seems unable to cooperate with others; is argumentative over every innovation.	Often fails to cooperate and is frequently disagreeable; difficult to get along with.	Gets along well with others much of the time; is occasionally obstructive.	Usually cooperates very well; willing to try new methods.	Works effectively with co-workers and supervisors; falls in readily with new ideas; gets along very well with others.

Remarks:

3. JOB KNOWLEDGE

Does employer know the requirements of job; the methods, systems and equipment pertaining to job?

No Opportunity To Observe ☐

UNSATISFACTORY	MARGINAL	GOOD	VERY GOOD	EXCELLENT
Does not know enough about most phases of job.	More knowledge of some phases of the job would be desirable.	Knows job well enough to get along.	Thorough knowledge of practically all phases of the work.	Has excellent mastery of all phases of the work.

Remarks:

4. INITIATIVE

Consider ability to proceed with job without being told every detail; to be generally resourceful; to get along without constant supervision.

No Opportunity To Observe ☐

UNSATISFACTORY	MARGINAL	GOOD	VERY GOOD	EXCELLENT
Routine worker; usually waits to be told what to do; needs constant supervision.	Often at a loss in other than routine situations; frequent checkup.	Does regular work without waiting for directions; requires some supervision on anything new.	Resourceful; needs minimum supervision; alert to opportunities for improvement of work.	Always gets on with the job on his own, seeks and sets for himself additional tasks; highly ingenious.

Remarks:

5. INDUSTRY

Consider the extent to which employee applies self to the duties of the job.

No Opportunity To Observe ☐

UNSATISFACTORY	MARGINAL	GOOD	VERY GOOD	EXCELLENT
Soldiers on the job whenever possible. Frequent socializing.	Frequently neglects his work.	Usually sticks to the job but with occasional wandering.	Conscientious most of the time but sometimes needs reminder to get on with his work.	Can always be relied upon to get things done.

Remarks:

6. QUANITY OF WORK

Disregard quality; consider only volume produced.

No Opportunity To Observe ☐

UNSATISFACTORY	MARGINAL	GOOD	VERY GOOD	EXCELLENT
Very slow; never turns out job on time.	Below average in output.	Turns out required volume, seldom more.	Above-average producer.	Unusual output; exceptionally fast; does more than is expected.

Remarks:

7. ABILITY TO LEARN

Consider the ease and speed with which employee grasps instructions and new methods; follows directions; remembers and applies new knowledge..

No Opportunity To Observe ☐

UNSATISFACTORY	MARGINAL	GOOD	VERY GOOD	EXCELLENT
Unable to grasp without constant re-instruction.	Learns slowly but usually remembers well or seems to grasp quickly but can not retain what she has learned.	Learns moderately fast and remembers with occasional check with supervisors.	Learns fast; remembers well.	Unusually quick and complete grasp.

Remarks:

8. ATTENDANCE

Consider the regularity and punctuality with which employee reports to work.

No Opportunity To Observe ☐

UNSATISFACTORY	MARGINAL	GOOD	VERY GOOD	EXCELLENT
Excessively absent or tardy.	Frequently absent or tardy.	Occasionally absent or tardy.	Rarely absent or tardy—then only for good cause.	Never absent or tardy.

Attendance Record for Rating Period _____ Times Tardy _____ Excused Absences _____ Unexcused Absences _____

(continues)

SUPERVISOR'S COMMENTS

Overall Evaluation = Score/2

Unsatisfactory (1–20)	Marginal (21–40)	Good (41–60)	Very Good (61–80)	Excellent (81–100)

Major Weak Points: _____   Major Strong Points: _____

_____   _____

What further training would be helpful to this employee? _____

_____

Does employee seem to be suited for this job?   ☐ Yes   ☐ No

If not, what would be better? _____

_____

Has employee taken any schooling after work in order to better himself or herself? _____

What company-sponsored training or activities has employee participated in? _____

_____

Additional Comments: _____

_____

EMPLOYEE'S COMMENTS

What can I as your supervisor do to help you to do a better job and improve yourself in the future?

_____

_____

Can you offer any constructive criticism regarding your job, your supervisors, or working conditions

in general? _____

_____

What other jobs or training do you feel you would be interested in that would afford you opportunity

for advancement? _____

_____

Additional Comments: _____

_____

Rated By _____   Date _____   Date Discussed with Employee _____

Reviewed By _____   Date _____

IMPORTANT: *This is your opinion of this employee's performance over the past review period. He will gain a better understanding only if you have communicated with and listened to him frequently during this period.*

Remember: *Strive for a better understanding between the employee and yourself. Clarify your mutual objectives. Be sure review is job oriented rather than personality oriented. Listen. Indicate your satisfaction in areas in which he has been effective. Reach an understanding of how the performance can be improved and establish a determination to improve it.*

Example 4

This form has some strong features and some weak ones. On the good side, three simple rating categories are described for Part II of the form: below requirements, meets requirements, and exceeds requirements. (I'd like to see another category here called *outstanding*.) Supporting statements are requested of the supervisor, and strengths and improvement needs must be identified.

On the negative side, major end results must be described by the supervisor in order of importance. This probably requires much time, effort, and frustration on the part of the person who develops the tasks. Much training would be required to implement this form. Also, there is no reference to what can be done to improve performance.

PERFORMANCE APPRAISAL

NAME _____

POSITION _____

DEPARTMENT _____

DATE OF EMPLOYMENT _____

DATE ENTERED PRESENT POSITION _____

INSTRUCTIONS

1. ACCOUNTABILITIES

List in Section I each of the accountabilities—or major end results—expected of the individual being evaluated. Depending upon the specific position, there are typically 3 to 8 major position accountabilities. List them in order of importance, from the most important to the least important.

2. EVALUATION OF ACCOUNTABILITIES

In Section II, perform an annual evaluation of the employee's progress toward fulfilling the requirements of each accountability by checking the appropriate box. Note that there are three boxes provided, labeled "Exceeds Requirements," "Meets Requirements," and "Below Requirements."

3. SUPERVISOR'S SUPPORTING STATEMENTS

In Section III, briefly discuss the employee's performance on each accountability and explain how each evaluation was determined. Give examples where possible.

4. ADDITIONAL COMMENTS

The three items presented in Section IV should be answered as completely as possible.

5. OVERALL EVALUATION

In Section V, make an overall evaluation of the employee's performance by considering the evaluation of each separate accountability and the data presented in Section IV. Assign a rating from 1 to 5. In general, those rated 1 and 2 combined would represent the upper 20%, those rated 3 would represent the middle 60%, and those rated 4 and 5 combined would represent the lower 20%. The definitions provided on the rear cover are designed to assist you in making your evaluation.

6. CAREER PLANNING

The two items related to Career Planning presented in Section VI should be answered as completely as possible.

7. COMPLETED EVALUATION

Both the employee and the supervisor should sign the completed evaluation form.

I. MAJOR END RESULTS
(Rank in order of importance.)

1.

2.

3.

4.

5.

6.

7.

8.

(continues)

II. SUPERVISOR'S RATING			III. SUPERVISOR'S SUPPORTING STATEMENTS (Give examples where possible.)
EXCEEDS REQUIREMENTS	MEETS REQUIREMENTS	BELOW REQUIREMENTS	

IV. ADDITIONAL COMMENTS

Summarize the employee's major strengths. _____
_____

Summarize areas for improvement. _____
_____

Describe additional factors that favorably or adversely influence the evaluation of this individual.
_____

V. OVERALL EVALUATION
(Place check on scale).

```
|_____||_____||_____||_____||_____|
    1         2            3              4         5
```

DEFINITIONS: PERFORMANCE LEVELS

1 = OUTSTANDING	Outstanding performance is that which is consistently characterized by work of exceptionally high quality.
2 = VERY GOOD	Very good performance is that which is noticeably better than that usually expected in the position.
3 = GOOD	Good performance is that which meets the requirements of the position in a consistently satisfactory manner.
4 = ADEQUATE	Adequate performance is that which usually meets the minimum requirements of the position but where performance may leave something to be desired.
5 = NEEDS IMPROVEMENT	Performance is inadequate and performance requirements are not being met.

VI. CAREER PLANNING

1. Does this person have an interest in other positions or types of work? If so, what are they? _____
_____

2. What further training and development is appropriate for this individual? _____
_____

This appraisal has been reviewed and discussed with the employee.

_____   _____
    Date   Employee's Signature

_____   _____
    Date   Supervisor's Signature

_____   _____
    Date   Manager's Signature

Example 5

This simple form breaks down the employee's job into sixteen different segments, which helps to pinpoint the specific factors to be judged. The descriptions help to clarify the factors but fall far short of standards. The three categories of appraisal are simple and quite descriptive.

This type of form may be useful in an organization that is not paper-work oriented. It might also be helpful where managers are not going to spend much time on performance appraisal because they are too busy meeting production schedules. Though it won't achieve the results that could be accomplished by the approach recommended in this book, it sure beats nothing. The form helps to communicate how an employee is doing and at least suggests job segments to be improved. Finally, it lends itself very well to a self-appraisal.

APPRAISAL OF SUPERVISORY PERFORMANCE

Name of Supervisor _____ Title _____

POSITION PERFORMANCE

Job Segment	Description	Strong	O.K.	Weak
1. Job Knowledge	Knows jobs of people supervised.			
2. Planning and Organizing	Develops and organizes plans and schedules.			
3. Delegation	Delegates work to qualified employees.			
4. Induction	Orients and inducts new employees.			
5. Training	Trains, coaches, and develops subordinates.			
6. Responsibility	Cares for equipment, tools, materials, and so on.			
7. Record Keeping	Maintains adequate records and reports.			
8. Empathy	Knows people personally, puts self in their shoes.			
9. Sociability	Gets along with people, is well liked.			
10. Discipline	Enforces rules and regulations, handles grievances.			
11. Judgment	Makes proper decisions, solves own problems.			
12. Follow-Through	Follows through on plans and assignments.			
13. Cooperation	Cooperates with other departments and with management.			
14. Production	Gets out work on time.			
15. Quality	Maintains high-quality standards.			
16. Costs	Holds costs down.			

Form Completed by _____ Date _____

Example 6

This form has many positive features. First, it has identified the major segments of the job. Although standards have not been established, the descriptions of each rating convey quite clearly the performance to be evaluated. And the instructions suggest that the manager should compare each employee to the same standard. The form offers some practical help for appraising and interviewing. It also suggests that an employee development plan should be prepared with the employee.

The problem with this form is that the form itself requires little time and effort to complete. To implement the many suggestions on the instructions would require much initiative, time, and paperwork on the part of the manager, and most of the time it won't be done.

PERFORMANCE EVALUATION

INSTRUCTIONS TO THE RATER

PURPOSE OF PERFORMANCE EVALUATION

To review individual's performance of presently assigned duties and responsibilities, to communicate performance expectations, and to discuss individual's future career plans.

SET THE DATE FOR PERFORMANCE EVALUATION CONFERENCE

Set the date, time, and place for the performance evaluation conference with the employee, preferably at least a week in advance.

Ask employee to review the "Employee Guide, Performance Characteristics Evaluation" to prepare for the conference. The employee may be given a copy of the evaluation form.

EVALUATE EMPLOYEE PERFORMANCE

Review employee's responsibilities as noted on your copy of the Position Description. If appropriate, revise the Position Description.

Reflect on employee's performance since the last evaluation.

COMPLETE PERFORMANCE EVALUATION FORM

Study each characteristic carefully before rating the employee. Evaluate each of the characteristics separately.

Compare each employee rated to the same standard. At no time should prejudice, partiality, or other factors influence the rating. Each employee's progress, or lack of progress, between each period of evaluation should be measured.

Modify the qualifiers for each performance characteristics, if necessary, by striking or adding words, as long as the general intent remains the same.

Write any comments in the space provided. If more space is needed, attach additional sheets that are adequately identified.

Give the employee an overall performance evaluation.

With the employee, prepare an employee development plan to correct areas in need of improvement, to improve skills needed for the current job, and to develop the skills needed for the employee's career advancement.

CONDUCT PERFORMANCE EVALUATION CONFERENCE

Meet alone with employee.

Solicit employee comments and questions.

Review employee's duties and responsibilities, resolving any misunderstandings.

Comment on employee's strengths, areas in need of improvement, and ways to improve job performance.

Review Performance Evaluation form.

Answer any questions.

INSTRUCTIONS

Send the WHITE copy to the Personnel Office. The YELLOW copy is kept by the supervisor, and the PINK copy will be kept by the employee.

(continues)

EMPLOYEE PERFORMANCE AND DEVELOPMENT REPORT
BASED ON PERFORMANCE DURING PERIOD
FROM _____ TO _____

_____   _____
Name of Employee (First, Middle, Last)   Civil Service Title

_____   _____
Division   Department

PERFORMANCE CHARACTERISTICS: Check the statement for each characteristic that most appropriately describes the employee. *YOU MAY CROSS OUT OR ADD WORDS TO MODIFY THE PERFORMANCE CHARACTERISTIC AS LONG AS THE BASIC INTENT REMAINS THE SAME.*

PRODUCTIVITY: Measure the volume of work accomplished and rate of progress on assignments.
- ☐ Fast worker. Rate of progress on assignments and volume of output is above average. Well organized.
- ☐ Work output satisfactory. Works at a steady pace. Work done timely.
- ☐ Works slowly. Only occasionally is output considered average.
- ☐ Very slow worker. Quantity of output is well below average of others in the same class. Does not utilize time effectively.

JOB KNOWLEDGE: Evaluate the employee's ability to grasp the procedures, techniques, Instructions of the job and the degree to which requires skills have been mastered.
- ☐ Has thorough knowledge of all aspects of work assignments and performs with high degree of skill.
- ☐ Has sufficient knowledge of duties and responsibilities of the work to satisfy requirements of the job. Degree of skill is met in most respects.
- ☐ Learns work assignments slowly. Requires much instruction and guidance. Attainment of required skills is marginal. Needs further training.
- ☐ Demonstrates little or no understanding of work assignments and seems unable or uninterested in mastering the skills required.

QUALITY OF OUTPUT: Evaluate the accuracy, thoroughness and appearance of work assignments.
- ☐ Work frequently incomplete or needs to be done over. Often repeats same kind of mistakes. Work is sloppy in appearance and poorly arranged.
- ☐ Work not completely unsatisfactory, but generally substantial improvement is necessary.
- ☐ Work is usually neat and presentable. Seldom needs major redoing. Seldom repeats mistakes. Generally adheres to applicable instructions.
- ☐ Work is complete, attractively presented, and accurate.

ATTITUDE: Consider interest and enthusiasm in work, reactions to constructive criticisms, support of management policies, reaction to supervisor's instructions.
- ☐ Demonstrates sustained motivation to do the best possible job.
- ☐ Reasonably conscientious and generally enthusiastic in performing assigned tasks. Makes an effort toward overcoming difficulties and volunteers when assistance is sought.
- ☐ No real interest in job. Satisfied to do the minimum.

HUMAN RELATIONS: Consider employee's ability to maintain harmonious working relations with others, both within and external to work unit.
- ☐ Has trouble getting along with others. Makes little or no attempt to improve person-to-person working relationships.
- ☐ Usually gets along with others.
- ☐ Very effective in meeting and dealing with others.
- ☐ An asset to the image of the work unit or office. Considerate of others' views and interests. Elicits cooperation from among others in the unit.

ATTENDANCE AND DEPENDABILITY: Consider whether the employee can be relied upon to appear for work on time and to meet work schedules.
- ☐ Extremely conscientious in meeting work schedules and in fulfilling responsibilities and commitments. Attendance is excellent and can always be depended upon for appearing and getting job done, regardless of circumstances.
- ☐ Can usually be depended upon to meet schedules and commitments. Makes effort to be punctual and to complete assignments on schedule. Seldom absent or tardy and reports absences and tardiness in advance.
- ☐ Occasionally is late in reporting to work or in keeping appointments. Requires more supervision than should be necessary.
- ☐ Can seldom be relied upon to meet work schedules without constant supervision. Frequent tardiness and apparent abuse or misuse of leave privileges. Does not usually report leave in advance.

RESOURCEFULNESS: Consider the employee's determination and energy displayed in overcoming obstacles within scope of the job, in finding solutions to problems, and in keeping productively occupied.
- ☐ Generally initiates action and finds solutions to problems. Makes creative and innovative contributions to work.
- ☐ Displays considerable energy and moves ahead on own initiative to complete assignments. Demonstrates resourcefulness and originality.
- ☐ Occasionally takes initiative in the performance of assigned duties.
- ☐ Usually relies on others to find solutions to problems.
- ☐ Almost never initiates action on the job without specific instructions. Work effort stops when an obstacle is encountered. Doesn't seek assistance.

Evaluate Employee's Overall Performance

☐ Outstanding   ☐ Very Good   ☐ Competent   ☐ Improvement Desired   ☐ Unacceptable

SUPERVISOR'S COMMENTS _____

_____

_____

EMPLOYEE'S COMMENTS _____

_____

_____

_____

_____
Supervisor Making Report

_____
This report was discussed with me

Example 7

This form combines the writing of goals and achievements with the checking of boxes regarding specific aspects of performance. It requires the manager to use the position description to clarify the prime responsibility results. General statements instead of standards of performance are used to explain the factors being rated.

The degrees of performance range from *poor* to *superior,* with *average* in the middle. The word *average* should not be used because it suggests a comparison with other people instead of evaluating the performance against a standard.

This type of form requires much thought, time, and effort to fill out. Managers would need careful training in how to use it effectively.

PERFORMANCE APPRAISAL

ADMINISTRATION/MIDMANAGEMENT/PROFESSIONALS

NAME

JOB TITLE

DEPARTMENT

EVALUATION PERIOD FROM _____

TO _____

JOB DESCRIPTION ☐ ATTACHED ☐ UNDER REVISION, WILL BE FORWARDED

I. RESULTS ACHIEVED LAST YEAR

Summarize the results achieved for each major goal established last year. Attach a copy.

GOAL #1   ☐ Met   ☐ Failed to Meet

GOAL #2   ☐ Met   ☐ Failed to Meet

GOAL #3   ☐ Met   ☐ Failed to Meet

GOAL #4   ☐ Met   ☐ Failed to Meet

GOAL #5   ☐ Met   ☐ Failed to Meet

II. EMPLOYEE APPRAISAL

PRIME RESPONSIBILITY RESULTS—To what degree the responsibilities listed on position description were fulfilled.

☐ Superior   ☐ Outstanding   ☐ Average   ☐ Acceptable   ☐ Poor

EVALUATION COMMENT: _____

_____

_____

MANAGEMENT SKILLS—Effectiveness in planning, organizing, leading, and controlling.

☐ Superior   ☐ Outstanding   ☐ Average   ☐ Acceptable   ☐ Poor

EVALUATION COMMENT: _____

_____

_____

COMMUNICATIONS—Degree of effectiveness of both oral and written communications.

☐ Superior   ☐ Outstanding   ☐ Average   ☐ Acceptable   ☐ Poor

EVALUATION COMMENT: _____

_____

_____

INTERPERSONAL RELATIONS—Success in dealing with supervisors, subordinates, peers, and other business contacts.

☐ Superior   ☐ Outstanding   ☐ Average   ☐ Acceptable   ☐ Poor

EVALUATION COMMENT: _____

_____

_____

DECISION MAKING AND JUDGMENT—Effectiveness in analyzing problems and determining appropriate actions.

☐ Superior   ☐ Outstanding   ☐ Average   ☐ Acceptable   ☐ Poor

EVALUATION COMMENT: _____

_____

_____

INITIATIVE & CREATIVITY—Ability to initiate action, develop new ideas, and handle unusual work situations.

☐ Superior   ☐ Outstanding   ☐ Average   ☐ Acceptable   ☐ Poor

EVALUATION COMMENT: _____

_____

_____

(continues)

(II. CONTINUED)

ADAPTABILITY—Consider ability to cope with change.

☐ Superior   ☐ Outstanding   ☐ Average   ☐ Acceptable   ☐ Poor

EVALUATION COMMENT: _____

_____

_____

_____

_____

III. SUMMARY

Change in overall performance level since last appraisal dated _____

☐ Improved   ☐ Same   ☐ Less Effective

Considering all the items discussed in this appraisal and any others you feel are important, summarize your assessment of this staff member's total effectiveness on the job. Specifically comment on the conditions influencing the environment in which the job was performed, i.e., degree of challenge presented. Also comment on the manner in which results were achieved, noting how the staff member's methods impact others in the organization, i.e., the degree of support given others.

_____

_____

_____

_____

_____

_____

_____

_____

_____

_____

_____

_____

_____

_____

_____

_____

_____

_____

_____

_____

IV. NEGOTIATED GOALS FOR NEW YEAR

GOAL #1

    DETAIL _____

_____

_____

    EXPECTED RESULTS _____

_____

_____

    ANTICIPATED OBSTACLES IN ACHIEVING _____

_____

_____

    HOW WILL THEY BE RESOLVED? _____

_____

_____

GOAL #2

    DETAIL _____

_____

_____

    EXPECTED RESULTS _____

_____

_____

    ANTICIPATED OBSTACLES IN ACHIEVING _____

_____

_____

    HOW WILL THEY BE RESOLVED? _____

_____

_____

GOAL #3

    DETAIL _____

_____

_____

    EXPECTED RESULTS _____

_____

_____

(continues)

(GOAL #3 CONTINUED)

ANTICIPATED OBSTACLES IN ACHIEVING _____
_____
_____

HOW WILL THEY BE RESOLVED? _____
_____
_____

GOAL #4

DETAIL _____
_____
_____

EXPECTED RESULTS _____
_____
_____

ANTICIPATED OBSTACLES IN ACHIEVING _____
_____
_____

HOW WILL THEY BE RESOLVED? _____
_____
_____

GOAL #5

DETAIL _____
_____
_____

EXPECTED RESULTS _____
_____
_____

ANTICIPATED OBSTACLES IN ACHIEVING _____
_____
_____

HOW WILL THEY BE RESOLVED? _____
_____
_____

V. PERFORMANCE IMPROVEMENT

List those areas in which you feel the staff member should work in order to improve effectiveness on the job, and recommendations for specific actions you would like to encourage the staff member to take to improve performance.

AREA	ACTION FOR IMPROVEMENT

ONE-OVER-ONE

_____   _____
Appraiser's Signature   Reviewed by Appraiser's Manager

_____   _____
Date   Date

COMMENTS OF ONE-OVER-ONE REVIEWER (OPTIONAL)

STAFF MEMBER'S COMMENTS

Each staff member is encouraged to express views on the fairness and accuracy of this Performance Appraisal.

_____   _____
Staff Member's Signature   Date

Example 8

This is a complicated approach that requires much time and writing. It also requires extensive training so that reviewers have the necessary understanding and skills to implement it effectively.

A number of positive features are included, such as the identification of strengths, job segments needing improvement, and specific action plans.

EMPLOYEE PERFORMANCE PLANNING AND EVALUATION

CONFIDENTIAL

EMPLOYEE NAME (LAST, FIRST AND INITIAL)				DATE OF PERFORMANCE PLAN	
POSITION PLAN				DATES OF PROGRESS REVIEWS	
DATE EMPLOYED	DATE ASSIGNED PRESENT POSITION	DATE ASSIGNED TO THIS SUPERVISOR			
COMPANY	DIVISION	LOCATION	DEPARTMENT		
				DATE OF PERFORMANCE EVALUATION	

(continues)

PERFORMANCE PLANNING

RESPONSIBILITIES* (Major headings of job responsibilities.)	PERFORMANCE FACTORS AND/OR RESULTS TO BE ACHIEVED A specific statement of the goals employee can reasonably be expected to achieve in the coming period for each responsibility. Indicate how results will be measured. When specific quantitative indicators are not possible, state the conditions that exist when a job is well performed.	PRIORITY** AND/OR TARGET
CHANGES IN PERFORMANCE PLAN—Use this section for any changes in plans before the end of the PPE period.		

PERFORMANCE EVALUATION

LEVEL OF ACTUAL ACHIEVEMENT	ADDITIONAL SIGNIFICANT ACCOMPLISHMENTS
	_____
	_____
	_____
	_____
	CONTINUING RESPONSIBILITIES Indicates additional responsibilities whenever they have had a significant positive or negative effect on the overall results achieved.
	RELATIONSHIP WITH OTHERS (JOB RELATED) Give <u>significant</u> positive or negative influence this employee has had on the results achieved by other employees.

OVERALL RATING

Review actual level of achievement against overall performance plans. Consider performance in key results areas, that is, actual performance against important priorities, dates, amounts and other factors listed above. Check the definition that best describes the employee's overall performance.

☐ Results achieved were unsatisfactory—performance did not meet expectations and must improve.

☐ Results achieved were acceptable—performance met expectations in most key results areas

☐ Results achieved were satisfactory—performance exceeded expectations in a few key results areas

☐ Results achieved were above average—performance exceeded expectations in many key results areas

☐ Results achieved were outstanding—performance exceeded expectations in most key results areas

*ALL MANAGERS ARE EXPECTED TO INCLUDE EEO, OSHA, AND EMPLOYEE DEVELOPMENT RESPONSIBILITIES AS AN INTEGRAL PART OF THE PERFORMANCE PLAN.

**USE THE FOLLOWING CODES TO CLASSIFY PRIORITIES:

A—MOST IMPORTANT   C—IMPORTANT
B—VERY IMPORTANT   D—OPTIONAL

NOTE: • TARGET REFERS TO COMPLETION DATES, AMOUNT, ETC.

• TRANSFER RATING TO EDR FORM TEN 4788.

(continues)

COUNSELING SUMMARY

    EMPLOYEE STRENGTHS: _____

_____

_____

    DEVELOPMENT NEEDS: _____

_____

_____

SIGNIFICANT INTERVIEW COMMENTS

Record additional significant items discussed by you or the employee during the Development/Evaluation interview.

_____

_____

_____

_____

_____

_____

_____

_____   _____   _____
(Manager's Signature)   (Print Name)   (Date of Interview)

EMPLOYEE REVIEW

The employee should use the space below to express any agreement or disagreement concerning the Performance Plan and/or Evaluation if he/she wishes to do so.

_____

_____

_____

_____

I have reviewed this Performance Plan and/or Evaluation with my manager. My signature means that I have been advised of my performance status and does not imply that I agree with this evaluation.

_____   _____   _____
(Employee's Signature)   (Print Name)   (Date)

MANAGEMENT REVIEW

Optional Comments _____

_____

_____

_____

_____   _____   _____
(Reviewer's Signature)   (Print Name)   (Date)

EMPLOYEE DEVELOPMENT REPORT

A. PERFORMANCE PLANNING AND EVALUATION

1. HOW DID YOU RATE THIS EMPLOYEE'S OVERALL PERFORMANCE DURING THE LAST PERIOD (TRANSFER RATING FROM TEN 4789):

   ☐ Results achieved were unsatisfactory—performance did not meet expectations and must improve.

   ☐ Results achieved were acceptable—performance met expectations in most key results areas

   ☐ Results achieved were satisfactory—performance exceeded expectations in a few key results areas

   ☐ Results achieved were above average—performance exceeded expectations in many key results areas

   ☐ Results achieved were outstanding—performance exceeded expectations in most key results areas

2. DATE OF RATING: _____

3. WHAT IS THE BASIS FOR YOUR OVERALL RATING? (INCLUDE SPECIFIC RESULTS THAT THE EMPLOYEE ACHIEVED AND USE ADDITIONAL SPACE ON BACK IF NEEDED.)

   _____
   _____
   _____
   _____
   _____

B. DEVELOPMENT PLANNING

1. DEVELOPMENT NEEDS
   WHAT EDUCATION, PERSONAL IMPROVEMENT, SPECIAL IMPROVEMENTS, OR OTHER FUNCTIONAL/DIVISIONAL EXPERIENCES WOULD IN-CREASE EMPLOYEE'S POTENTIAL FOR ADVANCEMENT AND/OR IMPROVE PERFORMANCE IN CURRENT POSITION?

   _____

2. ACTION PLANS
   WHAT SPECIFIC ACTIONS ARE PLANNED TO MEET THESE DEVELOPMENT NEEDS? WHEN? WHOSE RESPONSIBILITY TO IMPLEMENT?

   _____

3. PREVIOUS ACTION PLANS
   WHAT SPECIFIC RESULTS WERE ACHIEVED UNDER THIS EMPLOYEE'S DEVELOPMENT PLAN FOR THE PRIOR PERIOD?

   _____
   _____

(continues)

C. POTENTIAL FOR PROMOTION

1. EMPLOYEE'S INTEREST AND ASPIRATIONS (BASED ON EMPLOYEE'S VIEW AND COMMENTS TO YOU IN YOUR ONGOING RELATIONSHIP.)

_____

2. WHAT INDICATIONS DO YOU HAVE THAT THE EMPLOYEE IS CAPABLE OF ACCEPTING MORE RESPONSIBILITY?

_____

3. IN WHAT AREAS DOES THE EMPLOYEE HAVE POTENTIAL FOR ADVANCEMENT?

_____

4. PROMOTABILITY (HOW DO YOU RATE THE EMPLOYEE'S PROMOTABILITY?)

☐ Employee is not promotable at this time for one of the following reasons:
- *☐ Was promoted/transferred to present job _____ months ago. (i.e., has potential, but needs further experience on present job).
- ☐ Must achieve specific development goals before being considered for promotion.
- ☐ Personal (i.e., health, interest, family/relocation problems). Please indicate: _____

*☐ Employee has potential for one or more positions.
*☐ Employee has outstanding potential for one or more positions.

If the employee has potential for promotion (*ratings) please specify the positions for which employee should be considered: (consider other locations, Divisions, and/or affiliated companies): _____

• HOW DOES EMPLOYEE FEEL ABOUT RELOCATION? (CONSIDER FAMILY AND OTHER COMMITMENTS.) _____

REVIEWER'S COMMENTS

_____

(X) _____
(REVIEWER'S SIGNATURE)

_____
(PRINT NAME)

_____
(DATE)

D. REPLACEMENT PLANNING

PLEASE REVIEW EACH ITEM BELOW AND CHECK AND COMPLETE THE REPLACEMENT STATUS FOR THE EMPLOYEE BEING RATED.

☐ QUALIFIED REPLACEMENT—EMPLOYEES IN MY AREA OF RESPONSIBILITY AND QUALIFIED TO REPLACE THE EMPLOYEE BEING RATED ARE:

_____

☐ 18-MONTH REPLACEMENT—EMPLOYEES IN MY AREA OF RESPONSIBILITY WHO CAN BE DEVELOPED INTO A "QUALIFIED REPLACEMENT" THROUGH A PLANNED PROGRAM IN 18 MONTHS OR LESS ARE:

_____

☐ NONE—NO EMPLOYEE IN MY AREA OF RESPONSIBILITY IS "QUALIFIED" OR AN "18-MONTH REPLACEMENT."

☐ POSSIBLE REPLACEMENT—EMPLOYEES OUTSIDE MY AREA OF RESPONSIBILITY WHO MIGHT BE "QUALIFIED" OR 18-MONTH REPLACEMENTS ARE: (CONSIDER OTHER LOCATIONS, DIVISIONS, AND/OR AFFILIATED COMPANIES.)

COMMENTS _____

_____

_____

REPORTER
SIGNATURE: (X) _____ _____
(DATE)

PRINT NAME: _____

Example 9

This form requires the managers to establish their own standards and appraise performance against these standards. It leaves too much to the individual appraiser and requires much writing.

It isn't clear whether each factor should be rated from *poor* to *superior* or whether the reviewer should simply describe the performance. The only specific rating required is for overall performance. This may be sufficient for salary administration purposes, but it is unsatisfactory if improved performance is the objective. The word *average* should not be used.

A great deal of communication and training is required for this approach, and the results may not warrant the time and effort.

PERFORMANCE APPRAISAL

Employee's Name _____ Job Title _____

Department _____ Evaluation Period From _____ To _____

Job Description   ☐ Attached   ☐ Under Revision, will be forwarded

REVIEW THE STANDARD JOB DESCRIPTION WITH THE EMPLOYEE.
Summarize the specific duties of the job and establish expected standards.

_____

_____

_____

_____

_____

_____

_____

_____

_____

Does the employee understand the responsibilities and results?   ☐ Yes   ☐ No

CONSIDER THE FOLLOWING AREAS CAREFULLY AND DISCUSS EACH WITH THE EM-
PLOYEE. Be specific in your description. Keep in mind the job to be performed and the
standards of performance desired.

How does the employee's work measure up to your standards in terms of the following?

1. THOROUGHNESS, ACCURACY, AND NEATNESS. Consider work organization and appearance.

   _____

   _____

   _____

2. AMOUNT OF SATISFACTORY WORK ACCOMPLISHED. Consider quantity, quality,
   and ability to complete tasks.

   _____

   _____

   _____

3. EMPLOYER AND STAFF RELATIONSHIP. Consider salesmanship, service, enthusiasm, courtesy and cooperation.

_____

_____

_____

4. KNOWLEDGE OF THE JOB. Consider comprehension and acceptance of counseling, guidance, procedures, rules and regulations.

_____

_____

_____

5. OTHER ATTRIBUTES OR SKILLS NECESSARY IN THIS JOB. (If additional room is required, please attach a sheet to this appraisal.)

_____

_____

_____

OVERALL PERFORMANCE. Carefully review each of the five areas discussed and given an overall rating on the employee on the following scale.

Poor	Acceptable	Average	Outstanding	Superior

Comments on overall rating.

_____

_____

_____

PROGRAM OF DEVELOPMENT
1. WHAT HAS BEEN DONE SINCE THE LAST APPRAISAL INTERVIEW?

_____

_____

_____

_____

_____

_____

_____

_____

_____

(continues)

2. DESCRIBE THE NEW PROGRAM OF DEVELOPMENT AND WHAT PLANS HAVE BEEN DISCUSSED. BE SPECIFIC.

_____

_____

_____

_____

_____

_____

_____

_____

3. INDICATE THE EMPLOYEE'S REACTION TO THIS APPRAISAL. Indicate reaction to counseling session and employee's goals or aspirations.

_____

_____

_____

_____

EMPLOYEE'S COMMENTS, IF ANY

_____

_____

_____

_____

_____

This appraisal was
reviewed with me on: _____

Employee's Signature: _____

Appraiser's Signature: _____

Reviewed by Appraiser's
Manager: _____

Example 10

This complicated approach requires much writing. It combines responsibilities with objectives in one column and asks for comments in the next column. This is more confusing and less beneficial than identifying job segments and standards and then using specific ratings.

Although the general content of the form is satisfactory, and although there is a section on plans for improvement, too much writing and initiative are required of the appraiser. This makes the form impractical. This approach could not be used for self-appraisal.

STEP I. POSITION RESPONSIBILITIES & OBJECTIVES—PERFORMANCE RATING

NAME _____   LOCATION _____

JOB TITLE _____   DEPARTMENT _____

List the principal responsibilities for which the individual is accountable and the specific objectives that were established for the appraisal period.	Comment on the individual's discharge of responsibilities and attainment of objectives. Explain special difficulties, changes, etc. that affect accomplishment.

OVERALL EVALUATION OF ACCOMPLISHMENTS

Evluate overall performance of position responsibilities and objectives by checking one of the following:

OUTSTANDING ☐   GOOD ☐   ADEQUATE ☐   UNSATISFACTORY ☐

STEP II. EVALUATION OF MANAGERIAL ABILITY

Comment briefly on use of managerial skills and demonstrated leadership ability.

Consider such factors as: Knowledge of job . . . Control of expenditures . . . Communications . . . Teamwork . . . Delegating responsibility . . . Assuming responsibility . . . Planning and organizing . . . Contributing workable ideas . . . Making decisions . . . Relations with others . . . Training and development of employees. (Use specific examples, when possible.)

STEP III. SELF-DEVELOPMENT ACTIVITIES

1. What is the person's attitude toward self-development? Does he or she have a real desire to improve and broaden capabilities?

   _____

   _____

2. List the special training and development activities, inside and outside the Company, which the individual has engaged in during the past year.

   _____

   _____

3. List the individual's participation in professional, civic, and community activities. Indicate whether the individual provided leadership in these areas.

   _____

   _____

(continues)

STEP IV. PLANS FOR IMPROVEMENT

As the last phase of planning future job performance, supervisor and employee will develop specific plans to help the individual improve his or her perform-ance and encourage personal department. Consider actions by the individual and actions by you as the supervisor. Indicate any training programs and re-lated activities in which he or she should participate.

If the appraisal is limited because the individual is new on the position, check here: ☐

Appraisal Period: FROM _____ TO _____

APPRAISED BY:

_____   _____
           (Immediate Supervisor)   (Date)

_____   _____
           (Next Higher Supervisor)   (Date)

Performance discussion held with individual on _____
                                                    (Date)

SUMMARY—PERFORMANCE & POTENTIAL

NOTE: This summary is confidential and should not be discussed with the individual appraised. It is to be completed by the supervisor after the discussion with the individual concerning plans for improvement of future job performance.

SUMMARY EVALUATION—PRESENT PERFORMANCE

1	2	3	4
OUTSTANDING (Overall performance is clearly exceptional)	EXCEEDS REQUIREMENTS (Very good)	MEETS REQUIREMENTS (Satisfactory performance)	UNSATISFACTORY

FUTURE POTENTIAL

☐ 1. No indication of growth potential beyond present job.

☐ 2. Is ready for more responsibility and/or promotion.
   If so, to what specific positions—what greater responsibilities?

   _____

   _____

☐ 3. Will be ready for more responsibility and/or promotion with further development and experience.
   If so, what specific experience and development is needed? Could then fill what position?

   _____

   _____

SPECIAL SKILLS AND AMBITIONS

1. What special skills and talents does the individual possess?

   _____

2. Indicate the individual's ambitions within the Company. Does he or she have interest in other types or areas of work within the Company?

   _____

   _____

   _____

   _____

   _____

(continues)

HEALTH

1. Does health affect present performance? If so, explain.

_____

_____

2. Would health be a factor in a position of increased responsibility?

_____

_____

GENERAL

1. Particular individuals, for good reasons, may be giving only mediocre performance today. This may be due, for example, to age, health, or inability to adjust to change. Does this individual fall into this category? If yes, explain and recommend action to be taken.

_____

_____

_____

_____

2. Add additional pertinent comments, including significant events that occurred during the discussion of planning future job performance.

_____

_____

_____

_____

_____

_____

_____

_____

_____

Example 11

This form has many positive features. Although specific standards are not used, the descriptions of each job segment help to clarify what is expected as the basis for appraisal. Additional comments are encouraged. The five ratings are described in detail so that objectivity is encouraged. (See the performance category definitions following the form itself.) This form lends itself to a self-appraisal.

Its weakness is its lack of emphasis on and specific guidelines for improved performance.

EMPLOYEE PERFORMANCE REVIEW
(Nonexempt Salaried Employees Only)

Name	Dept. No.	Hired Date

Job Classification Title	Salary Grade	

Rate the employee on each of the factors below by placing an X in front of each factor that most closely describes the employee being rated. Should a particular description fail to adequately describe the employee's performance, feel free to delete or add words as appropriate.

QUANTITY OF WORK

_____ High-volume producer; frequently does more than is expected or required.
_____ Turns out satisfactory volume of work; occasionally does more than is required.
_____ Output is generally satisfactory but requires occasional prodding; does only what is required.
_____ Very slow worker; output consistently low.

QUALITY OF WORK

_____ Consistently produces error-free work; work is always neat and orderly.
_____ Usually produces error-free work; work is usually neat and orderly.
_____ Generally produces satisfactory work both as to accuracy and neatness.
_____ Room for improvement; errors frequent, work requires checking and re-doing.

RELIABILITY

_____ Always gets the job done on time; excellent attendance and tardiness record; dependable under pressure.
_____ Usually gets the job done on time; seldom absent or tardy; works fairly well under pressure.
_____ Performs satisfactorily; requires occasional prompting and checks on performance; generally satisfactory attendance record.
_____ Reluctant to accept responsibility; frequently careless or forgetful; frequently absent or tardy; fails to complete work on time.

INITIATIVE

_____ Displays unusual drive and perseverance; anticipates needed actions; frequently suggests better ways of doing things.
_____ A self-starter; proceeds on own with little or no direction; makes some suggestions for improvements.
_____ Does not proceed on own but waits to have procedures outlined; seldom makes suggestions for improvements.
_____ Continually needs prompting to complete assignments; never makes suggestions for improvements.

UTILIZATION OF TIME

_____ Always on the job; looks for additional work; does not distract others.
_____ Usually on the job; generally does not distract others.
_____ Easily distracted; room for improvement
_____ Spends too much time off the job; disturbs others.

JUDGMENT

_____ Uses exceptionally good judgment and makes sound decisions.
_____ Handles most situations well and makes sound decisions under normal conditions.
_____ Uses questionable judgment at times; room for improvement.
_____ Uses poor judgment in dealing with people and situations.

JOB KNOWLEDGE

_____ Expert in job; has thorough grasp of all phrases of job; seldom requires assistance or instruction.
_____ Understands and performs most phases of job well; occasionally requires assistance and instruction.
_____ Limited knowledge of job, further training required; frequently requires assistance and instruction.
_____ Inadequate; lacks basic understanding of job; constantly requires assistance and instruction.

ADDITIONAL FACTORS

Please comment on factors such as clerical skills, technical proficiency, attendance, or personnel relationships that have an important effect on employee's performance. If appropriate, make recommendations or suggestions for future personnel action.

Considering the specific ratings given above, indicate an overall performance rating of either:

(1) Marginal   (2) Fair   (3) Competent   (4) Commendable   (5) Exceptional

OVERALL PERFORMANCE RATING _____

| Date | Reviewing Supervisor | Date | Approved By |

PERFORMANCE REVIEW DISCUSSION WITH THE EMPLOYEE

Performance Review discussed on _____ by _____
                                                                          Supervisor's Signature

                                                                          _____
                                                                          Employee's Signature

Employee's Reaction to the Performance Review Discussion:

(continues)

Expanded Definitions of Performance Categories

Marginal—1
Use of this performance category implies:

- Has been on the job long enough to have shown better perform-ance. Probably should be told time is running out.
- Is creating a bit of a morale problem with those who have to help carry his or her load (including yourself).
- Just doesn't seem to have the drive or the know-how to do the job. Would be better off on some other job for which qualified.
- The employee's work is holding up that of the other positions with which it interrelates.
- It is more than likely that the employee probably recognizes that the job is not getting done.
- If performance continues at this level, the employee should be replaced.
- Just doesn't seem to get things accomplished.
- The work keeps falling behind. If you keep the employee much longer, you will be in real trouble.
- Seems to make one mistake after another; some of them are repeats.
- Apparently does not have the background to grasp the work.
- You have had adverse comments from outsiders concerning the employee's performance.

Fair—2
Use of this performance category implies:

- This employee is doing the job reasonably well. Performance meets the minimum requirements for the position and many of the normal performance requirements.
- The employee's performance is not really poor, but if *all* your people were at this performance level, you would be in trouble.
- You would like to see the employee improve, but in the mean-time you really don't have too much to complain about.
- May be the kind of employee who needs some pushing and fol-low-through, but does the job under close guidance.
- You may have to keep a close watch; otherwise, you would con-sider the employee competent.

- The employee shows drive but needs to acquire more know-how.
- You may have to plan the employee's programs or assignments step by step. After that, the job usually gets done.
- Some of your employees have to "carry" the employee on occasion.
- Can't always depend on the employee to complete the assignments or the daily work unless you keep checking.

Competent—3
Use of this performance category implies:

- This employee is doing a full, complete, and satisfactory job. Performance is what is expected of a fully qualified and experienced person in the assigned position.
- You would not require significant improvement. If improvement *does* occur, it's a plus factor for your group's effectiveness. If it *does not,* you have no reason to complain.
- If all your employees were as good, your total group's performance would be completely satisfactory (in your judgment and your manager's, too).
- You get few complaints from others with whom the employee's work interfaces.
- Errors are few and seldom repeated.
- Demonstrates a sound balance between quality and quantity.
- Does not spend undue time on unimportant items, neglecting problems or projects that should have priority.
- You feel reasonably secure in quoting the employee's input or recommendations.
- Requires only normal supervision and follow-up and usually completes regular work and projects on schedule.
- Has encountered almost all the activity fields of the position and has proved quite capable in each.
- You consider the employee a good, solid member of your team and feel reasonably secure in making any kind of an assignment within the scope of the job and level.

Commendable—4
Use of this performance category implies:

- This employee exceeds position requirements even on some of the most difficult and complex parts of the job. Takes the initia-

(continues)

tive in development and in implementation of challenging work goals. Normally, this individual would be considered for promotion.

- You are getting *more* than you bargained for.
- You find the employee accomplishing *more* than you expect.
- Is able to take on extra projects and tasks without defaulting in other assigned activity fields.
- Each project or job tackled is done thoroughly and completely.
- The employee's decisions and actions have paid off to a higher degree than would be expected.
- Often provides "extras."
- Requires only occasional supervision and follow-up.
- Frequently exceeds objectives.
- Does own advance planning, anticipates problems, and takes appropriate action.
- Shows a good grasp of the "big picture." Thinks beyond the details of the job, and works toward the overall objectives of the department.
- "If you had four like this employee, you would only need three."

Exceptional—5
Use of this performance category implies:

- Employee demonstrates a knowledge that normally can be gained only through long periods of experience in this particular type of work.
- Recognized by all as a real expert in this job area.
- This employee can usually be a prime candidate for promotion when a higher-level position in this or a related field becomes open.
- The employee's actions show an understanding of work well beyond the assigned area. Outsiders seek the employee out because of knowledge of *many* facets of the department's work.
- Requires little or no supervision or follow-up.
- Shows unusual initiative and is a self-starter.
- Almost invariably takes the best approach to getting the job done.

Note: This level of performance must be looked at in terms of both *quantity* and *quality.* Use of this category shows that you are recognizing really outstanding worth to the company within the level of this position.

Example 12

On the positive side, this form is simple to understand and easy to complete. It is very much oriented toward behavior and lends itself well to a self-appraisal.

On the negative side, nothing is included about the identification of strengths or weaknesses. Also, there is no form or procedure for planning and implementing improved performance.

EMPLOYEE JOB PERFORMANCE EVALUATION

Department: Production

Employee's Name: _____

Job Title: Shop Foreman   Date: _____

Instructions: Immediately to the left of each job behavior is a line on which you are to indicate the level of performance. Enter a numerical value on each line, indicating one of the following:

$$+2 \quad \text{Superior}$$
$$+1 \quad \text{Commendable}$$
$$0 \quad \text{Good}$$
$$-1 \quad \text{Marginal}$$
$$-2 \quad \text{Unsatisfactory}$$

Job Behaviors

_____ Carries out work as directed by Production Manager.
_____ Plans and supervises shop work.
_____ Assists with monthly inventory.
_____ Spot-checks craftsmanship on finished products.
_____ Supervises truck loading and unloading.
_____ Makes out bills of lading.
_____ Maintains storage areas in good condition.
_____ Enforces safety rules and regulations.
_____ Monitors for efficient use of materials.
_____ Trains new employees.
_____ Works well with employees.
_____ Meets production standards.
_____ Repairs salvageable materials when practical.
_____ Organizes work efficiently.
_____ Interviews and screens job applicants.
_____ Maintains high morale among employees.
_____ Motivates employees to higher productivity.
_____ Employs and terminates shop employees with discretion.
_____ Is flexible.
_____ Maintains shop in cleanliness and in order.

Comments: _____

_____

_____

From Robert W. Carsell, *Evaluation Dynamics* (Columbia, S.C.: The Interaction Press, 1979).

Example 13

This form is simple to understand and administer. It would be appropriate for a self-appraisal, and it is job oriented.

The word *average* is used, which will confuse the appraiser because of the dual standard of the job and other people. No forms or procedures are included for improving performance.

PLANNING	RATING

1. Does employee set both short-term and long-term goals for the department unit in verifiable terms (either qualitative or quantitative) that are related in a positive way to those of his or her manager and company? _____

2. To what extent does he or she make sure that the goals of the department are understood by employees? _____

3. How well does he or she assist subordinates in establishing verifiable and consistent goals for their operations? _____

4. To what extent does he or she utilize consistent and approved planning premises and see that employees do likewise? _____

5. Does he or she understand the role of company policies in decision making and ensure that employees do likewise? _____

6. Does he or she attempt to solve problems of employees by policy guidance, coaching, and encouragement of innovation, rather than by rules and procedures? _____

7. Does he or she help employees get the information they need to assist them in their planning? _____

8. To what extent does employee seek out applicable alternatives before making a decision? _____

9. In choosing from among alternatives, does he or she recognize and give primary attention to factors that are limiting, or critical, to the solution of a problem? _____

10. In making decisions, how well does he or she bear in mind the size and length of commitment involved in each decision? _____

11. Does he or she check plans periodically to see if they are still consistent with current expectations? _____

12. To what extent does he or she consider the need for, as well as the cost of, flexibility in arriving at a planning decision? _____

13. In developing and implementing plans, does he or she regularly consider longer-range implications of decisions along with the shorter-range results expected? _____

14. When submitting problems to a manager, or when a manager seeks help in solving problems, does this employee submit considered analyses of alternatives (with advantages and disadvantages) and recommend suggestions for solution? _____

RATINGS

5.0 = *Superior:* a standard of performance that could not be improved upon under any circumstances or conditions known to the rater.

4.0 or 4.5 = *Excellent:* a standard of performance that leaves little of any consequence to be desired.

3.0 or 3.5 = *Good:* a standard of performance above the average and meeting all normal requirements of the position.

2.0 or 2.5 = *Average:* a standard of performance regarded as average for the position involved and the people available.

1.0 or 1.5 = *Fair:* a standard of performance that is below the normal requirements of the position, but one that may be regarded as marginally or temporarily acceptable.

0.0 = *Inadequate:* a standard of performance regarded as unacceptable for the position involved.

From Harold Koontz, *Appraising Managers as Managers* (New York: McGraw-Hill, 1971).

Example 14

This form has good features. First of all, ten significant job segments are listed. Although no standards were established, the various appraisal terms (unsatisfactory, marginal, and so on) are defined. Space is allowed for remarks, and the form lends itself nicely to a self-appraisal.

The main weakness of the form is its lack of emphasis and specifics in terms of development of the employee.

PERFORMANCE — Engineering Personnel Annual Appraisal

1 QUALITY OF WORK

UNSATISFACTORY	MARGINAL	ACCEPTABLE	COMMENDABLE	OUTSTANDING
Poor quality of work, continually makes errors, requires excessive checking and rework.	Careless, inclined to make mistakes, work barely acceptable.	Meets minimum requirements of accuracy and neatness, average quality of work, needs normal supervision.	Exceeds minimum requirements of accuracy and neatness, very few errors, carries out instructions well, needs little supervision.	Consistent high degree of accuracy and neatness, work can be relied upon, very little rework, seldom needs supervision.

REMARKS: _____
_____
_____

2 ATTENDANCE

UNSATISFACTORY	MARGINAL	ACCEPTABLE	COMMENDABLE	OUTSTANDING
Often absent or tardy. Does not report absence or tardiness in advance. Very undependable.	Erratic in attendance and punctuality. Seldom reports absence or tardiness in advance. Not dependable.	Occasionally absent or tardy. Reports absence or tardiness in advance.	Seldom absent or tardy. Always reports absence or tardiness in advance. Dependable.	Excellent attendance record. Always at work and on time. Very dependable.

REMARKS: _____
_____
_____

3 JOB KNOWLEDGE

UNSATISFACTORY	MARGINAL	ACCEPTABLE	COMMENDABLE	OUTSTANDING
Definite lack of knowledge. Very little understanding of job duties. Needs considerable instructions.	Inadequate knowledge of duties. Understanding of job duties not sufficient.	Has adequate knowledge of duties. Needs a little additional instruction.	Good knowledge of duties. Well informed. Occasionally needs direction.	Excellent understanding of job assignments. Requires very little direction. Extremely capable.

REMARKS: _____
_____
_____

4 ATTITUDE

UNSATISFACTORY	MARGINAL	ACCEPTABLE	COMMENDABLE	OUTSTANDING
Difficult to work with. Chip on shoulder attitude. Uncooperative. Rude.	Occasionally unwilling to follow orders without argument. Inclined to be stubborn.	Tries to cooperate. Usually agreeable and obliging.	Cooperative most of the time. Interested in work. Quick to offer assistance.	Always cooperative. Shows a high interest in work. Goes out of way to help. Pleasant.

REMARKS: _____
_____
_____

5 QUANTITY OF WORK

UNSATISFACTORY	MARGINAL	ACCEPTABLE	COMMENDABLE	OUTSTANDING
Slow worker. Does very little work, wastes time.	Works at a slow pace. Needs encouraging and urging.	Works at a steady pace. Meets minimum requirements.	Works fast. Often exceeds requirements.	Very fast and prompt worker. Consistently exceeds requirements.

REMARKS: _____

_____

_____

6 VERSATILITY

UNSATISFACTORY	MARGINAL	ACCEPTABLE	COMMENDABLE	OUTSTANDING
Seems unable to learn new tasks. Cannot adjust from one job to another. Resists change.	Learns new tasks slowly. Has difficulty in understanding and going from one assignment to another.	Neither slow or fast. Able to perform several related tasks. Handles new alignments with some difficulty.	Catches on fast. Learns new tasks easily. Handles new assignments with minimum amount of difficulty.	Very adaptable and flexible. Masters new tasks easily. Handles various assignments without difficulty.

REMARKS: _____

_____

_____

7 PLANNING

UNSATISFACTORY	MARGINAL	ACCEPTABLE	COMMENDABLE	OUTSTANDING
Is very poorly organized.	Poorly organized. Just gets job duties completed.	Makes some mistakes, but generally is organized in completing tasks.	Very seldom makes mistakes. Most of the time is well organized in completing tasks.	Hardly ever makes a mistake. Always well organized in completing duties.

REMARKS: _____

_____

_____

8 INITIATIVE

UNSATISFACTORY	MARGINAL	ACCEPTABLE	COMMENDABLE	OUTSTANDING
Never volunteers to undertake work. Requires constant prodding to do work. Has no drive or ambition.	Needs some prodding to do work. Dislikes responsibilities. Has very little drive. Believes in just getting by.	Seldom seeks new tasks. Will accept responsibilities when necessary but does not go out of way. Routine worker.	Occasionally seeks new tasks. Works well when given responsibility. Makes occasional suggestion.	Definitely a self-starter. Goes out of way to accept responsibility. Very alert and often constructive.

REMARKS: _____

_____

_____

(continues)

9 **CREATIVITY:** Consider whether subject has evidenced imagination and ingenuity in solving problems that accompany job responsibilities.

UNSATISFACTORY	MARGINAL	ACCEPTABLE	COMMENDABLE	OUTSTANDING
Rarely contributes any new ideas or suggestions.	Occasionally contributes some new adaptation of established principles or procedures.	Has been alert to find better ways to carry out responsibilities.	Readily produces new solutions to problems and evidences ingenuity in solving them.	Has produced unique solutions to problems that have application in or beyond the area of job responsibility.

REMARKS: _____

_____

_____

10 **PERSONAL APPEARANCE**

☐ **Needs Improvement**
☐ **Satisfactory**

This quality refers to the employee's personal grooming, attire, and overall appearance. Does the employee's personal appearance meet the standards for the job? An employee's attire is usually dictated by the nature of his/her work, which should be consistent in evaluating this quality.

_____
Signature of Supervisor

_____
Interview date

The above rating has been reviewed with me.

_____
Signature of employee

11 **DISCUSSION**

A **What does employee feel is necessary to improve his/her efficiency?**

_____

_____

_____

_____

B **Is employee satisfied with his/her job?**

_____

_____

_____

_____

C **What can/should be done to improve employee's value as a ▮▮▮▮ employee?**

_____

_____

_____

_____

D **Goals:**

_____

_____

_____

_____

E **Additional comments:**

_____

_____

_____

_____

Example 15

This set of forms illustrates the principles described in this book. It begins with a blank form that can be used in any department. The specifics in the first two columns (significant job segments and standards of performance) must be developed by manager and employee. The appraisal headings are the ones suggested in this book: *does not meet standards, meets standards, exceeds standards,* and *outstanding.* A space for comments is also included.

The second form requires agreement on outstanding performance and performance needing improvement. The development of a specific performance improvement plan is then required for one or possibly two performance areas needing improvement.

The final form is to be completed by the manager. It may or may not be communicated to the employee.

NAME _____

SUPERVISOR _____

DATE _____

APPRAISAL OF JOB

SIGNIFICANT JOB SEGMENTS	STANDARDS OF PERFORMANCE (What conditions will exist when the job is done in an acceptable manner?)

Significant job segments are discussed between employee and manager to reach under-standing and agreement.

Standards of performance are developed to correspond with the significant job segments of Column 1.

Appraisal is made on the basis of standards of performances.

Comments should explain ratings given.

(continues)

PERFORMANCE   **APPRAISAL**

	Does not meet standards	Meets standards	Exceeds standards	Outstanding	COMMENTS

**Appraisal Summary and
Performance Improvement Plan**

I. SUMMARY OF PERFORMANCE APPRAISAL

A. Outstanding Performance (Order of Priority)

1.

2.

3.

B. Performance Needing Improvement (Order of Priority)

1.

2.

3.

II. PERFORMANCE IMPROVEMENT PLAN

Training Need* _____

Action to Be Taken	By Whom	By What Date

*It is strongly suggested that you concentrate on only one need at a time. If you are working on two needs that may be closely related, attach another sheet of paper to this form.

(continues)

JUDGMENT OF PROMOTABILITY

I. OVERALL PERFORMANCE ON PRESENT JOB
(See copy of "Appraisal" form for a complete appraisal.)

☐ Outstanding   ☐ Good   ☐ Adequate   ☐ Unsatisfactory

II. PROMOTABILITY

A. Estimate of level

☐ 1. Has potential for promotion to two or more levels above present job.

☐ 2. Has potential for promotion to next higher level only.

☐ 3. Currently limited to present job.

☐ 4. Present level is too challenging.

B. Readiness for promotion (check only if A "1" or "2" was checked above).

☐ 1. Is ready for promotion now.
To what kind of job(s)?

☐ 2. Will be ready in two years or less.
What kind of training and experience are needed?

☐ 3. Will require more than two years.
What kind of training and experience are needed?

(Use back of page for additional comments.)

A Final Word

hope you found this book practical and interesting. Lots of ideas have been presented that remind me of a committee the American Management Association formed to define the word "management." It decided that "management' is a science and an art. It went on to explain that the "science" of management is "concepts, theory, principles and techniques." And that is what this book has presented from many sources.

The committee defined "art" as the application of the concepts, theories, principles and techniques. This means that your job is to select those ideas that you can use or adapt to your own situation.

If you are a line manager, look for ways of doing a better job of planning and conducting performance appraisals so that you end up with a "performance improvement plan" that you and your employee have developed together. Also, study the chapter on coaching and see what athletic coaches and others say are the characteristics of an effective coach. Choose those attributes that will help you get maximum performance from your employees.

If you are a human resources manager, analyze the forms and procedures of your performance appraisal program. Be sure you build into the process the objective of improving performance and not just making decisions on merit increases and promotion.

If you are a training professional, work with the human resources manager to develop a program for training the line managers to implement the program effectively. This means teaching them how to appraise, conduct an effective interview, develop a "performance improvement plan," and coach for improved performance.

Don't forget to complete the "posttest" (following Chapter 6) to challenge your opinions on performance appraisal and coaching, whether you are a line manager, a human relations director, or a training professional. If you did the pretest, compare your answers to see what you learned and/or just changed your mind.

Selected References

Following is a list of selected references. Each can contribute to your knowledge and skills related to improving employee performance through appraisal and coaching.

American Society for Training and Development. *How to Conduct a Performance Appraisal.* Alexandria, Va.: Info-Line Series, May 1990.

Berk, R. A. (ed.). *Performance Assessments: Methods and Applications.* Baltimore: Johns Hopkins University Press, 1986.

Bernardin, H. J., and R. W. Beatty. *Performance Appraisal: Assessing Human Behavior at Work.* Boston: Kent, 1984.

Cardy, R. L., and G. H. Dobbins. *Performance Appraisal: Alternative Perspectives.* Cincinnati: South-Western, 1994.

Falcone, Paul. *101 Sample Write-Ups for Documenting Performance Problems.* New York: AMACOM, 1999.

Grote, Dick. *The Complete Guide to Performance Appraisal.* New York: AMACOM, 1996.

Grote, Dick. *Performance Appraisal Question and Answer Book.* New York: AMACOM, 2002.

Hargrove, Robert. *Masterful Coaching.* New York: Wiley, 2003.

Kirkpatrick, Donald L. *Evaluating Training Programs: The Four Levels,* 2nd ed. San Francisco: Berrett-Koehler, 1998.

Latham, Gary P., and Kenneth N. Wexley. *Increasing Productivity Through Performance Appraisal,* 2nd ed. Reading, Mass.: Addison Wesley, 1994.

Lewin, D., J. B. Mitchell, and M. A. Zaidi (eds.). *Handbook of Human Resource Management.* Greenwich, Conn.: JAI Press, 1996.

Lloyd, S. Baird, Richard W. Betty, and Craig Eric Schneier. *The Performance Appraisal Sourcebook.* Amherst, Mass.: Human Resource Development Press, 1982.

Mohrman, Allan M., Susan M. Resnick, and Edward E. Lawler III. *Designing Performance Appraisal Systems.* San Francisco: Jossey-Bass, 1989.

Smither, W. (ed.). *Performance Appraisal: State of the Art in Practice.* San Francisco: Wiley, 1998.

Stone, Florence M. *Coaching, Counseling and Mentoring.* New York: AMACOM, 1999.

Swan, William S. *How to Do a Superior Performance Appraisal.* New York: Wiley, 1991.

Tornow, W. W., and M. London (eds.). *Maximizing the Value of 360° Feedback: A Process for Successful Individual and Organizational Development.* San Francisco: Jossey-Bass: 1998.

Index

About the Author

Donald L. Kirkpatrick holds B.A., M.A., and Ph.D. degrees from the University of Wisconsin in Madison. At the Management Institute of the University of Wisconsin, he taught managers at all levels the principles and techniques of many subjects, including human relations, communication, managing time, managing change, leadership, motivation, and decision making. In industry, he developed a Performance Appraisal System for International Minerals and Chemical Corp. Later he served as personnel manager of Bendix Products Aerospace Division.

He is a past national president of the American Society for Training and Development, which gave him its highest honor, "Lifetime Achievement Award in Workplace Learning and Performance," in 2004. He is a member of *Training* magazine's Hall of Fame.

He is the author of seven management inventories and seven management books, including *Evaluating Training Programs: The Four Levels,* which has become the basis for evaluation all over the world. He is a regular speaker at national conferences of ASTD, IQPC, and other professional and company conferences.

The first edition of this book received the "Best Book of the Year" award from the American Society for Personnel Administration (ASPA), now called the Society for Human Resources Management (SHRM).

To contact Don, e-mail him at dleekirk1@aol.com. For more information, visit www.donaldkirkpatrick.com.